Prologue

This amateur-authored story is about two friends doing their best to live a full life. Today's episode includes an unusual experience of *biking* outside of their comfort zone. It represents a leap of faith in ourselves, each other, our families, and mother nature.

The primary purpose of writing this is simply for my own recollection and, therefore, you'll have to excuse me if I don't describe some minutia fully (I've done my best to keep an audience in mind). I enjoyed the upcoming experience very much and hold it dear. When I'm old and long out of the saddle, I'd like to proudly read the story of a younger, bolder version of myself. A fortunate byproduct is that as generations seem to pass, it would appear that each generation needs something to point at to prove to their children that their parents are/were once cooler or more badass than their offspring might appreciate. So long as I am putting the effort into writing, perhaps you might find some fun in reading through our experiences.

While I may use some flair-ful phrasing, I stamp my approval of authenticity on this story. Nothing ahead is fabricated and I've done my very best to represent the reality of our time on the trail. That said, memory and cognition fades with the amount of physical effort we undertook, and I apologize in advance for any inaccuracy or the poor placement of a photo. I'll extend this to the dialogue included. It's close, but might not be exact.

A warning is in order for impressionable minds. When you're in the middle of nowhere, disconnected from society, some words get used that would be frowned upon at the dinner table! I've bleep-ed the worst ones, but who are we kidding? You can't just add symbols and not still think the word in your head. Parents, you've been warned.

Next, I like using sarcasm. And commas. And I only proofread this once. Deal with it.

Finally, I'd like to dedicate this to our families. I hope these memories justify that their sacrifices weren't taken for granted. The pages ahead hold the gifts of their willingness to play along with our project, and we are forever grateful.

The Beginning

Brad, my wife Jordan, Brad's wife Elissa, kiddo Kennedy, and myself; Left to right.

At the time we started getting the itch to complete a huge ride, my riding buddy and friend, Brad and I have been so for about three years. We met through mutual friends, and he, along with his wife Elissa and new kiddo Kennedy, became close friends to my wife, Jordan, and I. Since then we've shared a broad spectrum of experiences together from family dinner nights to camping excursions in Colorado and elsewhere.

Brad and I have been riding together for a long time. I think we end up riding with each other the most out of our friends. Brad rides well, really well. He downhills effortlessly. I can climb and eat and talk at the same time, but find it a real struggle to match Brad's downhill speed. Each rider has their specialty. My skill set comes with the requirement to not get knocked out due to my day job, therefore, I descend a little more gingerly. I imagine it's like being an aspiring race car driver who uses his track vehicle to get to work on Monday. Can't wreck the car, now, can we? Brad showed me the friendliness of introducing new trails to an out-of-towner. Since then, we've found a routine of riding in the foothills often, occasionally getting into the front range and alpine zone, and once-annually taken a trip out west to find the gems of the mountains further abroad. It has been a truly wonderful and diverse experience to have ridden so much with such a good friend and his friends.

One day we discussed our bucket list items of things we wanted to do. This wasn't just on the bike, but in general, a life-list. I think he mentioned first of doing a long trip on the bike. Combining backpacking and biking – bikepacking. I too had a desire to get a long, "real" trip of backpacking but hadn't considered the bike side. In the years leading to this moment I was losing hope and thought time was quickly passing to find a friend to commit to such a big adventure. Therefore, I was stunned with excitement to hear these words coming out of my close friend's mouth. I've been hungry for a decade waiting to go out and really adventure out of the comfort zone. I couldn't stop grinning as I realized that I may have just found the opportunity. I agreed that I had the same desire to get into the backcountry and find what we're made of in our own way. On a more personal side, I also had a desire to put my money where my mouth is on all of the adventurous talk and bravado that comes out of me. I wanted to see if I had the cojones to actually back up the life I project. Instagram versus reality. This challenge fit well to prove and learn many things about myself and my friend.

I should note that neither of us has attempted anything longer than about a three- or four-night *backpacking* stint. Neither of us has done any bikepacking at all. We both have extensive car camping experience with our bikes (shout out to Fruita and Moab).

We had a serious conversation over dinner and tossed around a few ideas of what ride should we target. The choice was quick and obvious:

The Colorado Trail

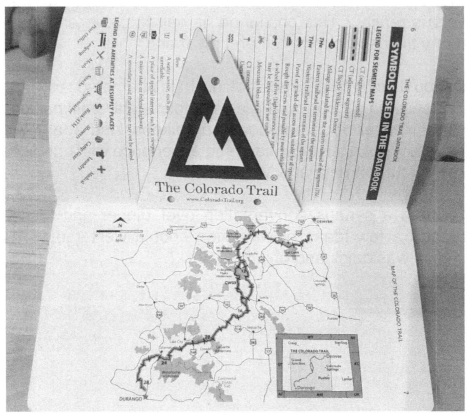

*A standard CT "blaze" and map of the Colorado Trail.
Courtesy of The Colorado Trail Foundation.*

It was very close to home (15 minutes driving to Waterton Canyon, the Northern Terminus), the timeline fit (about a two-week ride), the style of trail was a good fit (singletrack with alpine riding), and it appeared very challenging (our estimates were grossly inaccurate; it was extreme).

The Colorado Trail (CT) for bikers is approximately 540 to 550 miles of trail extending from Denver to Durango. It includes over 70,000 feet of climbing or elevation gain over those miles. That's *four times* the elevation gain from Everest's Base Camp to the summit. The average CT elevation is over 10,000 feet above sea level and the top reaches 13,271 feet. Slightly before the halfway mark, the trail splits with a choice of "Collegiate West" or "Collegiate East". The original trail follows the "East" route and is the required route for bikers. The "West" route was finished only in 2012 and provides an optional, up-close experience of the Collegiate Peaks mountain range. The West route is available to hikers only (see below). The trail lingers in the "Alpine Zone" for great distances, which just means the trail elevation is tickling or above the tree line, typically north of the 11,000-foot mark. The vast majority of the trail is spent on "singletrack", a trail wide enough for only one hiker or biker to travel on at a time. In the mix is also some "doubletrack", dirt roads, and paved roads. The latter two made up the vast majority of the Wilderness Area Detours.

Bikers can't participate in the entire continuous CT due to the trail passing through six "Wilderness Areas". These areas are protected from certain human activity to help provide a more pristine experience of nature...for humans. This protection extends well beyond the development of land and even includes "mechanized" travel or equipment. Not just cars or ATV's, either. A hunter cannot use a rolling game cart, and a forest worker cannot use a chainsaw, for example. When they say pristine, they mean it! The lawmakers, unfortunately, believe human-powered bikes fall into this category of mechanization and a rider cannot enter the area with a bike at all. Therefore, there are official, very circuitous, sometimes soul-crushing detours around some of the best sections of the actual Colorado Trail. Call your congressman.

The trail is broken into 28 segments where a user can find access to the CT by car, 4x4, hike-out, etc. Of the 28, a full 10 are required to be detoured if you travel by bike. While it is disappointing that a rider can't see the entire beauty of the trail, it does provide a valuable opportunity to resupply in many small cities. The trail itself passes Breckenridge, Twin Lakes, and the small Monarch Spur campground for supplies. The detours add the towns of Leadville, Buena Vista, and Silverton. Each of these places provided us with a well-deserved meal and resupply for the next round of battle with the peaks.

The trail passes through many historic areas and has its own rich history too. From mining areas, to military history, to geologic history, it was a great experience to literally bike through time. For those interested, more history of the trail itself can be found here https://coloradotrail.org/trail/trail-history/

Ready the Ship

Brad and I shook hands on the plan and walked away from that table feeling excited. I'd say we started to get serious about our preparation in the fall of 2018 and our original plan was leaving late July of 2019. We figured by then the trail would be well passable based on historical snowpack information and the temperatures would be pleasant in the alpine zones that cover the majority of the trail. We massaged our vacation time to accommodate the project, and I burnt both weeks of my annual vacation to do it (thank you, Jordan, for your tolerance). Using both weeks back-to-back is a huge sacrifice in my job but it is what the project demanded. I hope to make it up to Jordan soon and get out and travel somewhere warm.

Within those 6 or so months, I was promoted at work and had to reschedule my vacation time less than 3 months prior to leaving. Thankfully, Brad had the flexibility to accommodate my new mid-August vacation. In retrospect, we had one of the largest snowfall seasons on record and the trail may not have even been passable had we left on our original date. We also wouldn't have been nearly as prepared physically. Fate, baby, you can't stop it.

I went to the CT foundation page (https://coloradotrail.org) and purchased maps, the guidebook, the databook, and a poster of the route. Buying from their site also helps support the foundation. When they arrived, the planning began and didn't really stop until we left. Brad laid out the early goal of about an 11-day trip. One night together we hashed out a rough plan in the databook of what we'd like to accomplish each day. With this outline, I began to nitpick the details until my databook was so covered in notes, each segment's margin contained some morsel of additional information. I gathered information from hiking and bikepacking sites and apps such as COTREX and MTBProject, the CT Foundation page, and Facebook pages for the Colorado Trail Race and the CT Thru-Hikers pages. All of these provided useful data as well as real-time reports coming off the trail. I was making notes all the way up until the ride itself.

All kinds of things were considered. Mileage, elevation gain, elevation profile, possible campsites, water problems, food problems, longest stretches between ____, bailouts if need be, resupply box location, bike repair items, pack weight sheet, to-do lists, partner's to-do list, what worked for others, etc. etc. etc. I even prototyped and 3D-printed some parts to modify our tent system.

3D printed parts used on the ends of custom aluminum tent poles. This replaced the required hiking poles to support our tent.

Start planning early. It's labor-intensive and time-consuming. Ask my wife, she'll tell you.

Aside from the daily plan, we prepped our bodies and bikes as well. We felt that both needed to be in top form for the adventure or we'd only be sealing our likelihood of failure.

My wife, Jordan, is a personal trainer, nurse, and professional athlete. How convenient! She understood what was ahead more than I did. Two- and three-a-day training sessions for weeks of preseason are no stranger to her and she was clearly in her wheelhouse designing workouts for me. She attended to both the long slow-burn grind as well as maintaining my punch at altitude. Maybe most important, she educated me on *how to recover* each night and improvise those techniques in camp. She helped me eat well before the ride and suggest food options that would work on the trail itself to help combat the calorie deficit we'd be operating in.

I work on-call. During these times, I wait next to my phone and ponder the meaning of life most of the time. However, in the 6 months leading up to the ride, I was alternating between good, long, hard lifts or training bike sessions, and long runs. Between those workouts, I'd be over a bowl of honest-to-god healthy, organic, natural power food doing more planning and nitpicking of the data and trail reports. My days off of work I was riding long and often and prepping my bike and gear.

Time-consuming. Ask her.

My well-salted weight vest after a training ride near home

The Clydesdale
(Technical speak ahead, feel free to either skip to adventure or nerd out with me)

I ride a 2019 Spot Mayhem 130 29er, size large. Isn't it beautiful? It is a well-refined carbon frame full-suspension mountain bike and my prized trail companion. I, and more so Brad, considered picking up or building some hardtails for the ride itself. This was just one of the hundreds of things we had considered for the optimum chance of success. Eventually, we decided to follow the phrase we saw on bikepacking.com,

"The best bike to use is the one you already have. If you currently ride a mountain bike that works for you on the

trail, chances are it will make a very capable bikepacking rig with few modifications"

This indeed turned out to be true. I'm happy we didn't go for hardtails. I wasn't convinced about betraying my silky, trail-slaying mistress to ride some strange, inflexible street pickup. Yes, our rigs weighed more, yes, it introduced more complexity that could fail, yes, it reduced our storage capacity. It was well worth it for the taint protection, wallet protection, and most importantly, the downhill grins.

I saw a picture in which 2019 Colorado Trail Race *winner* Kurt Refsnider posed with his bike in front of the Waterton Canyon finish line. He finished in 4 days and 12 hours and *– oh damn, is that a full-suspension he's riding?* Who knew. Ride what you have my friends, it strengthens the bond.

My first temporary trail name was Clyde, because of the appearance of everything I carried on my bike! My actual trail name, Quasi, came later (we'll get to that). I wasn't actually carrying much more than Brad, but the *way* I was carrying it was cumbersome and unwieldy, especially compared to Brad's surprisingly succinct load appearance.

My planned loadout, still in 'shakedown' status.

With the plan to stick with our daily drivers (Brad rides a Yeti SB5 27.5), we started a bag plan. We wanted to keep the bikes skinny, so no paniers. I consider it uncommon now to find panniers on the CT (Although we did see a couple pushing monster fat bikes with huge, hard-sided panniers heavily-laboring up a very rocky climb). Obvious choices were a handlebar roll and a seat post bag. Complicated options were available for full-suspension frames. On the high end are custom fit, lifetime-quality bags from a place like Bedrock Bags. On the low end (that's us, baby; budget went in the bike) were closeout deals from Backcountry.com on a double set of Topeak Midloaders. We arranged them to hang on the downtube and *on top of* the top tube. This took some finesse but, in the end, it actually worked well for storage capacity and location. We complemented these with Topeak's reasonably priced handlebar roll and seat post bag, the

Frontloader and Backloader. Simple names for simple bags, and for a total of $230 a bike, dry bags included, our storage system was complete. Not terrible considering some of the prices we found that widened our eyes. This supplemented the hip packs and water bottles we already utilized on daily rides.

Next was modification and maintenance. I read a oneofsevenproject.com article about that rider's equipment choices and he mentioned he geared his bike down. Having the 70,000ft climb actively invading my nightmares, I followed suit and changed my 32t chainring to a 30t (~$33). Making the ratio 30x50 in my SRAM X01 drivetrain. Brad made a similar move and sourced a 28 tooth chainring resulting in 28x46 in his Shimano XT/SLX drivetrain. *Very* happy we did that, it might have made the difference between finishing or not.

The stock tires that came with my bike were worn and were not the combination I most enjoyed, so I switched to a Maxxis EXO DHF front, and EXO Aggressor rear in 2.3 (~$110 total). This is a common setup with many Colorado riders. In hindsight, the 2.5 WT size, what Brad rolled, would likely have been better. Someone on the trail also mentioned he would have put something "other than a single-ply tire" on. My bike nerd level doesn't cut deep enough to cross-reference tire ply layers by model with such on-sight rapidity, so I was blissfully unaware until he said that, around mile 400ish. I'd been running this combination for the last three years without a single flat in hard, front-range riding. I figured they passed the test well enough. More to come on THAT subject.

I utilize Ergon's GS1 grips (~$30). This came about after our move to Colorado. The joints in my fingers began to hurt so bad on jarring downhill descents that I'd have to pull over. The larger grip size and additional "shelf" to support my wrists eliminated this pain and I think this helped with the hours behind bars on the CT as well.

My chain was still in good shape from low miles since new. Brad's however, had not been changed in 1600 miles and was stretched way out of spec (lookin' at you, bud) so I immediately rectified that issue (I'm the maintenance guy of the two of us). This exposed that his cassette wore to the stretched chain and so we were forced to replace his cassette as well. For all you reading this, chains are $25, cassettes are not.

Brad's new cassette. New bike parts look so darn good!

We both removed our dropper posts and elected rigid aluminum seat posts (~$50). We had seat post bags and there was no room to drop the seat without the tire hitting the bag anyway. For those of you with internally routed cables, remember to run a string or other re-routing solution through your frame *as you pull your dropper cable out*. Use a piece of tape or something on the end of the cable. This is so you can thread that dropper cable back in yourself, easy-peasy.

Finally, Brad installed new brake pads, tires, and had his suspension serviced. We both bumped our suspension pressure for added frame weight we'd be carrying in supplies.

The Plan
(Trail and Food)

As our near-daily training sessions and rides continued, our actual plan of attack was getting more and more solidified. Or so we thought. I'll explain the plan we had, but the 10th Mountain Division of Segment 8-9 would echo, "No plan survives contact with the enemy". They're not wrong.

Our plan was to preposition my truck in Durango at a trail angel's house and we'd ride to the truck to drive home. After Brad got off work, we'd start with a short shakedown on Segment 1 the night of Wednesday the 14th and camp at the Platte River. We had a rough outline of the rest of the ride and how much we wanted to accomplish every day. This even included where we might want to camp each night. We figured we can crank out 25-mile sessions in 3 hours like we usually do on our big rides. Two big sessions a day should still leave us all kinds of extra time to chat, fish, journal, enjoy mountain towns, etc. At that rate, and with so much time to recovery every afternoon, we calculated a finish of 10, maybe 11 days.

Fools. We were such fools.

First modification: My wife (again, many thanks) insisted that she wanted to drive the 6 hours to pick us up in Durango and then the 6 hours home too. We thought this was an extremely generous offer and I could tell she wanted to be there for the finish and to see me again after the ride. I also cherished the idea of celebrating together at the finish too. However, Brad and I still felt she was really over-extending herself and my guilt of making her drive the 12-hour trip was overpowering my hopes that she would be at the finish. However, to drive the final nail into the issue, Jordan further added that this change would "provide you a way to bail-out of the trail with a call for pickup" if we found ourselves in that situation. Considering a bail-out was about a 50/50 chance, that comment changed our opinions almost immediately. Prior, if we bailed-out, we'd need to source a ride home to Denver *and then get my truck from Durango also!* Brad and I looked at each other and realized we'd been one-upped. Women. They can be so logical, dammit.

Return logistics in place, we had done some research into what foods can pack the most calories into each ounce carried up that 70,000 feet. We joked about guzzling olive oil and spreading lard on peanut butter. To start, we actually had a great menu of high-quality endurance fueling items. Jordan tailored many of my choices to some premium selections of hydration powder, energy butters and gels, protein sources, and carbs. The problem is, I simply didn't compute there'd be no way to source these premium picks further on the trail itself. I figured when we roll through a town, I'll pick up similar items. That was simply not the case. We planned for one box to be sent ahead to the Monarch Spur Campground near Monarch Pass. We included as many premium items as we could but couldn't help notice that gas stations along the way don't carry organic-non-GMO-clean-carb-complex-protein-such-and-such. So, our favorite *acquired* meal was instant bacon-bit mashed potatoes, with a packet of pink salmon on top, and plenty of salt. Ha! Other backpackers will know what I'm talking about---the red packets you can spot from across the store when you roll into town starving.

Food we brought or shipped from home that lasted the whole trip:

- High quality hydration powder - think Amazing Grass tablets or even Nuun Endurance products, not Gatorade mix.
- Coconut oil packets - this is great to mix into a hot dinner, great flavor boost and lots of calories.
- Nut butter packets - add to snacks or a meal. Many varieties, my favorite was RX Honey Cinnamon Peanut. Single-use, convenient and very packable.
- Pure honey - Sourcing actual pure honey can be deceiving, so I brought the good stuff.
- Instant quinoa bowls - repacked into vacuum-sealed sleeves with a $10 thrift store food saver.
- Protein powder - high-quality protein powder, chocolate flavor, in a Ziploc bag in my frame bottle. Great treat in the evening while recovering.
- Daily Vitamins - Multi, B, zinc, and fish oil.

Each town we rode through we smashed a huge, proper meal at a local joint. These tasted amazing, felt civilized, and were a great boost for the psyche. We restocked with local store or shop items that seemed commonly found for most of our journey.

Sourced food that worked:

- Fresh fruit and vegetables - Don't forget about eating fiber. Dense sludgy food for 3 days straight nearly ended my trip, see below.
- Dried fruits - Apricots were my favorite
- Instant.... anything - Mashed potatoes, macaroni, rice, backpacker meals, etc.
- Protein packets - Salmon, tuna, chicken, chili, you name it. If it fits, it ships and will go in my belly.

- 'Victory' Snickers - Pair these with a trail goal and they're twice as sweet
- Hard cheese wedges - The harder the better, they are a great snack and flavor boost
- Sauce packets - Olive oil, Taco Bell, Pesto, Mayo, Mustard, and so on
- Beef sticks over the counter - Fresh seemed tastier (We call them 'smokies' where I grew up)
- Doughnuts - In almost every grocery store or gas station, and always less than $1 each.

We loaded up our bikes and brimmed our bags full of calories. With all of the preparation complete, I think we both took one more long, hard, loving stare at our trusty rigs, as if to communicate our hope for them to last just 550 more miles, if no more after that. It's one of those look-back-at-your-work-before-turning-the-garage-light-off-and-going-to-bed moments.

And So, It Begins
(Segment 1)

Brad and I at the start of the CT. Notice Brad's more compact bag loadout at the time!

We started in the late afternoon on Wednesday, August 13th. Brad finished a half-day of work and I went over a few more things that probably didn't need going over at all. When the time came, we loaded up both of our monsters and my wife's bike, and made the short drive to Waterton Canyon.

Meeting at the Northern Terminus was a surreal moment. You could detect the energy between Brad and I, and the caution in Elissa and Jordan. I would sum it up in a phrase such as, "Well...I hope this works". We stood in front of the Waterton Canyon sign for a picture. You can see the mouth of the canyon, the canyon's waterworks equipment, and 550 miles of mostly unknown stories behind us. For this adventure I commissioned a new set of cheap workman's gloves, my favorite for dirty riding. I held up my hands with my fingers open and Jordan smiled. Written across the tanned leather palms read, "DURANGO BOUND" in black sharpie. I couldn't wait.

We had some laughs and good wishes and hugs and kisses. Brad had a moment with Elissa, their daughter Kennedy, and their unborn second before he, Jordan, and I passed the sign and rode up the canyon together. We had begun and the first 100 feet were behind us.

As we turned away from Elissa and Kennedy, I remembered an interaction we had about a week prior. Jordan and I were over for a framily dinner night, and I was trying to ask Elissa if, in the commotion of our preparation, we had missed anything that she needed before we left. She was lost for an answer for a moment, but narrowed down what she really needed.

"Survive", she responded.

In some way reminiscent of an old western, I wheelied my horse the best I could before we circled around and we three rode into the sunset. "We've got this", I was trying to say. I'm not sure if the message was received, I'm an old soul.

The mouth of the canyon squeezed the South Platte River and the smooth dirt road of the old South Park and Pacific railbed, and swallowed us and we rode. We'd been fishing and exploring up this canyon many times before but this time we knew we weren't coming back out (well, Jordan was). We passed all the spots of the river we'd enjoyed before and eventually stopped at the ranger station and Strontia Dam. Water shot intensely out of the dam's base as it usually does and fed the Platte River we'd been riding alongside.

Brad and I pose (like idiots) in front of Strontia Dam

Jordan and I hugged for a long time but reminded each other that we were going to be together soon. We'd planned a stop to meet with both our spouses again at Kenosha Pass and Breckenridge, only two or so days away. She took a few pictures of us before we left for good. Brad and I left her behind and pointed west into the first climb of Segment 1. It was on.

Jordan later told me a trail story of her own. She's particularly good at spotting bighorn sheep in the canyon and likes the challenge to find them. So, as she pedaled back down the easy, featureless, dirt road her eyes were up on the canyon walls doing what she does best. She hustled along at a fast clip but some movement caught her attention just in front of the bike. Her eyes met a large snake just as she was rolling over its tail! "My brain didn't even process it was a snake until it was too late. All I had time to do was lift my feet up and hope I didn't wrap it into the wheels!" Yikes! Maybe the snake has healed and there is another irate side of this story being told among the rocks there.

We started up the climb and Brad reminded me of the steepness of some of the sections ahead. I rarely remember the bad experiences of any trail (a gift and a curse) and almost didn't agree with his recollection. I recalled the lush green encroaching vegetation, the switchbacks down to the Platte river on the other side, and the killer downhill if you return to the canyon in the reverse direction. The laws of physics reminded me that to have a killer downhill meant we had to climb a dreadful uphill. And I remembered. This section took us longer than we imagined…. imagine that. We had to push over many of the uphill sections, even the ones we rode previously. The heavily laden bikes weren't convinced by our effort.

Gradually, during the climb, my brain became aware that something hurt. My left knee was bothering me a surprising amount. I was fuming and nervous. *Already? For f---- sake! How is this possible? Will it get worse? Will it end the ride on the first day?.* I think fear is controlled by your failure possibilities early in the trail, at least it did mine. I was more afraid that any little thing might come along and ruin the whole plan than I was for my safety. Here it was. First 15 miles.

We hit our first singletrack milestone at Lenny's Rest. It's not much, just a rough lumber bench with the vegetation cleared around it. It is a memorial to a young hiker who died in a hiking accident. The view is rather good despite the tight greens all around, and the mood of the place was warm, not sad as you might expect. It felt like a sanctioning of our ride.

My knee continued to strain as we finally crested our first peak in the trail around sunset. The process so far was working! We were a little clumsy on our awkward bikes. We found it would take time to become accustomed to the new weight distribution as our lean ladies rode a little more drunk than nimble. We pushed on to the descent and began to reap the rewards of our climb. We enjoyed this first downhill immensely. This time it was so different from all the other passes we'd made through this section. We played on the features of the trail all the way to the bottom. It wasn't long before the light became dim and we were checking on each other's vision. Brad shouted back to me, "How ya doing? Can you keep going? Seeing alright?" but an adjustment in speed took care of the lack of light just fine. It helped me see our first major hazard on the trail before we got in the danger zone.

I rolled over the crest of trail segment at moderate speed and directly in front of me, hogging the middle of the trail, was a genuine skunk! I stopped as fast as I could to keep out of his striking radius and was glad to find I was successful! We shooed him along as best we could but he wasn't a very receptive individual. We inched closer and closer and eventually he took off running on the path of least resistance---the trail ahead. For 20-freaking-minutes we followed this skunk as his tiny legs ran down the trail in front of us. He wasn't very quick and our light was already nearly gone. It became a ridiculous situation. We tried everything. We pushed a little closer and found he was already running at his maximum speed. We backed off a bit but he only took a break on the trail and went back to running. Eventually, after a silly amount of time, he was so exhausted he was stumbling over the obstacles ahead. He tripped, rolled, and recovered and, still in a panic, darted in the direction his body happened to pointed when he found his feet again. Luckily, this pushed him off the trail. We were free to descend at our regular pace. We laughed at the outrageousness of the situation as we finished up the remainder of the descent.

After a few more switchbacks and passing some other late-night hikers moving by headlamp, we started searching for a site to call home for the first night. We knew we were getting close to the Platte River and the guidebook said there were sites within a quarter mile of the end of the segment. We found a small grass and dirt area to our left and figured it was good enough. Something I hadn't anticipated was to share a camp space with neighbors. The trail was planned through such remote areas I thought it might be more than a day between human sightings in some spots (eventually it would be). Right in the area we chose was another camper, already buttoned up for the night. From inside their tent, a woman's voice said hello. We asked if they minded if we camped next to them and they said so long as we kept the noise down, they would not. We did our best but were laughing under our breath as we spread out for the night. Camping gear is made of some exotic materials and some of it crinkles worse than aluminum foil! We did our best to muffle our excited giggling about the day's events. We were making our first camp!

After we set camp, Brad suggested we walk down the trail to the river to filter water and clean up. We trotted a fair distance down the trail with our headlamps, water bags, and soap and passed a few more tents in other sites. I was surprised by how busy the end of Segment 1 was as we got closer to the river. There had to be eight or so tents scattered about. We filled both of our bags with some water for the night and got to the elephant in the room. How were we planning on "cleaning up"? We both looked at each other and my headlamp danced between Brad and the river. I concluded, "I think I'm just going to skinny dip it!". I tossed off my clothes and jumped in the Platte River. The water was warm and deep and the current manageable. It was an absolute delight. I floated on my back looking up at the stars and took in the moment. We'd finally made this wild idea happen. We were really here, really doing it, and I was completely thrilled. We washed up in a rocky and shallower section of the river, put our clean sleeping attire on, and headed back up the trail.

We didn't eat much that night. I had a Phat Phudge packet and we bagged the rest of our food. I wish you all could see the circus act that occurred next. We tried to do the right thing and hang our food bags in a nearby tree. Bears were reported in the area and we didn't want to offer any of our hard-moved food to the gods just yet. We searched by headlamp until we found a sturdy overhanging branch to throw a cord over. Trying not to wake our neighbors, I took a few attempts to toss the cord bundle over the top. Once we got the cord over the branch we started to pull the bags up, but the cord became twisted in the numerous pine fingers bristling off the branch. The bags were stuck high in the air, and releasing the cord did nothing to bring them back down. Our food was marooned 10 feet up. We died laughing at our bad luck, cussing under our breath. We tried to move the cord, tugging from many different angles, but it was of no use. Our solution: Brad climbed onto my shoulders to reach the branch height and tried to release the bags. So, there we were, night one, total darkness, working with two small light sources,

Brad wobbling on my shoulders with his hands high above his head doing his best to save all our food from being abandoned while trying to not make any noise. It was hilarious, and Brad was eventually successful. Our bear bag worked so well it was almost human-proof too.

After that calamity was over, we finally zipped up the tent and retired to our sleeping bags for our first night out. Neither of us was particularly tired as our spirits were very high. We were both riding a wave of optimism. We crinkled around on our sleeping pads until we got comfortable and drifted off.

Why We Love our Home Segments
(Segments 2-3)

Brad in front of the Gudy Gaskill Bridge about to cross the Platte River into Segment 2

It was a tough first night of sleep. I laid awake in the tent for a while trying to solidify the rush of emotions into my memory. The excitement was coursing through my body and made me smile in the intense black of the tent. My open eyes wandered around for something to see but failed in the darkness, and I felt like I'd made my bed in an empty alternate universe. Brad moved and crinkled his sleeping pad and snapped me out of it. After that drug wore off, getting used to the new bedroom made our sleep only on-and-off. It didn't matter, we were brimming with eagerness to get to work.

Segments 2 and 3 are classic local rides for us. We'd flown through these sections numerous times before and consider them some of our favorite backyard rides. I woke up at first light still eager to get moving. As I started to stretch in bed, I noticed my knee hadn't hurt like the night before. I smiled and sensed a wave of cautious optimism about this early problem. The more I moved, the more I sensed that it was in a far better state than yesterday when I fell asleep. Maybe it was just my mind convincing itself to ignore it. All I knew is that the game was definitely back on.

We packed up camp and rode down to the river again to have breakfast. On the way we passed the other hikers and campers who's tents we saw last night. Today, however, they were outside their mobile homes and packing up as we rolled by. We greeted each person we encountered and the mood on that slope was energetic. Everyone seemed happy and excited to start the day. The CT was already proving to be a special place for these kinds of interactions.

Down at the Platte River, we returned to the place we had washed up the night before. In the daylight, the view was far different from our limited experience last night. These canyon walls were tight and wrapped around to limit our view down the river to no more than a quarter mile in each direction. Brad started his camp stove and began heating a round of water. I cracked open some breakfast items and started to snack. We brewed some instant coffee and enjoyed a slow pace and our hot breakfast packets.

While we ate, we had a conversation with our camp neighbors from the night before. They applauded us on being so quiet! Brad and I looked at each other and almost busted up laughing. If only they knew of our bear-bag-three-ring-show from the night before! We asked a few questions that we would know to become common, "Where are you two from?", "How long are you planning on going?", "Are you resupplying anywhere?". I, for the life of me, can't remember any of their answers.

We finished breakfast and packed our trash away. We mounted our bikes and crossed the Gudy Gaskill bridge. This was a powerful moment for me. Gudy is the mother of the Colorado Trail and this bridge was built in her honor. She fiercely advocated for such a trail and was instrumental in its construction decades ago. I felt her smiling down on us as we rolled above the rapid waters below. Our late start will cost us on our ride today. Even as we started up the steeper climbs out of the canyon, we could feel the heat of the day coming on. We knew the sections ahead were hot and dry and we hoped that we could get through without too much misery. I think we underestimated the tax these sections would have because we had become so familiar with them. These first hot miles would hurt later in the day.

As we traveled along the single track we bobbed in and out of the Buffalo Burn areas of 1996. This huge fire has left the forest scarred with wide open views of treeless hills. This has always provided us with an awesome perspective on the area's size but today it also baked us on the exposed trail. The trail consists of very dry and scrubby trees and brush in all directions and parched grass filling the remainder of the view. On the horizon you can spot boulder peaks and low mountains in the distance. We rolled along this singletrack up and down the slopes of these mountains and flowed up and over all of the burnt hillsides. One of the neat spots in this segment is an abandoned quartz mine. Off the left of the trail you can see leftovers of white rock piles in otherwise amber-colored soil. If you decide to approach the old mine, you'll see a few old trucks and equipment pieces have been smashed into the mine's opening, sealing it forever. It almost feels like a black hole opened up inside and pulled everything around into the opening to plug itself off.

As we neared the end of Segment 2, we saw the fabled firehouse known to CT hikers. The CT databook marks this station as the first public water spigot on the trail. The firefighters are nice enough to provide an outdoor filling station on the back of this firehouse and all CT travelers are welcome to use it to better pass this arid section. I wondered if the amount of dehydration emergencies they were likely responding to nudged them to install it! We pulled in and filled our bags after a few other hikers finished up. That day, some firefighters were there working on equipment and we thanked them for the resource.

We finished Segment 2 in the Little Scraggy parking lot. Up ahead was one of our favorite sections of all time. Segment 3 is a fun, flowing, backcountry ride that we've enjoyed many times. As we rode, the trail darted in and out of the Buffalo Burn scar. This really is a treat because you change quickly between dry forest to open meadow. The trail is dirt covered in "kitty litter", decomposing granite that was exacerbated by the fire. As we rode through this section we passed the numerous side trails that we'd ridden before. This area is packed with riders on the weekends, but on weekdays, I've ridden as many as 30 miles through the backcountry areas and not seen another soul. No map was needed for this section, it was a blast of grip and rip on our home turf.

Despite our enjoyable time, this section provided me with my first glimpses of the plan not going to plan. The first part was my own poor planning. I had an entire additional pack I scavenged from an old backpack lid wrapped around my handlebars. I put extra camera mounts, our maps, things to do in camp, etc. in this floppy bag. While we traveled, I was constantly correcting its position on my handlebars and it became a real nag. It would flop over onto my front tire, drop onto my top tube, essentially go anywhere except where I wanted it on atop my handlebars. This culminated in ruining our favorite downhill of Segment 3. One section of the CT passes on a wild descent down a defunct 4x4 trail. The rain washouts and slope of the trail make for a high-speed full suspension workout with a few drops and jumps on the way down. Brad and I typically crush this section with a bro-five at the bottom, but my unruly bag put a stop to all of that. Halfway through the descent, in the essence of the entertainment, my bag flopped onto my front wheel and began jamming itself in. I tried to wrangle it while still on the move but was forced to stop, and Brad stopped behind me. He laughed and said he was wondering what the hell was going on up front. I tore the bag off my bars and wrapped it around my torso securing it above my primary hip pack. This added an extra hump to my silhouette and christened my trail name, *Quasi.*

Second, as we rode I realized our pace was slower than I think we both anticipated. I began to calculate the time it would take to arrive at our planned family meet at Kenosha Pass, and easily concluded that we'd be forced to ride well past the ending-hour that we estimated each day. Having a, *ahem,* conversation with Brad, we realized we didn't have a choice but to accept the longer days of riding. This took me a few days to come to grips with, but I was wrong and I'm thankful for what our pace ended up being. For those of you reading this, I'm saying I got frustrated because our progress was drifting from the schedule at such an early phase. After I admittedly focused my frustration at the only other human for 30 miles, I apologized to Brad at the time, and I hope he knows I'm still sorry for being a turd. I learned the error of my way later in the ride when it became clearly evident that the milder pace we delivered was actually one of a few key factors that allowed us to finish at all. The trail will become so difficult that maintaining the rate we both planned and trained for was absolutely impossible. Had we been firing at the originally planned speed, we would have had to bail. In fact, in the end I wish we had *more* time to spend on the trail to cut down on the gargantuan daily effort and sample some beer in town. So, Brad, that one's on me. I'm genuinely thankful for our reduction in pace and grateful you delivered the goods day after day out there.

We finished our descent and began to climb our way out of the Buffalo Creek area. Soon after we reached the end of Segment 3 when the trail met the graded dirt of Wellington Lake Road. To our right was the tiny village of Bailey, CO (although not tiny enough to be missing a brewery) and to our left was the recreation area of Wellington Lake. Thus, we began the first 80 miles of draining, mandatory detour.

An Introduction to Official Detours
(Lost Creek Wilderness Detour)

*A textbook example of the exposed and hot sandy roads
of the middle third of the detour*

The dirt road we now passed on was wide and mildly sloping, but the washboard bumps were intense. As cars' tires pass over the road and hit an imperfection, it compresses the tire which compresses its suspension. As the tire and suspension rebound back toward their normal position, that returning force creates another pressure point on the road beyond the first imperfection. Eventually, because the road is dirt and erodible/compressible, a second imperfection develops in that pressure point and continues the cycle until the entire freaking road looks like a perfect washboard. It's enough to rattle the fillings out of your teeth.

We gritted and laughed at the comedy of our shaking until we soon reached Wellington Lake. This lake is a privately owned, manmade body of water nestled in forested surroundings and nearby mountain peaks. It's generally a gorgeous area complete with a full campground and picnic tables surrounding the water's edge. We have spent an afternoon at the lake before and pulled out some killer fish. So, we rolled into the entrance of the lake to stop for lunch. When we asked the person behind the desk what they had for purchase, they replied, "We don't have any food here". Nothing?! This lake is so remote, it's a full 30 minutes *driving* on those same washboard roads to get to Bailey, the closest place that cooks a meal or provides any resupply. We were stunned and disgruntled. How can they not even have a cooler of Cokes?

We walked out of the 'welcome' office and back under the sun. Nearby, we dumped our bikes and gear at a picnic table near the water's edge and decided to pick lunch out of our bags. I remember eating off a block of cheese and pairing it with some crackers and honey. We chatted for a while and stretched. After filling our water bags in the lake, we mounted back up again and started off southbound on the detour. As we passed the lake on our right and were about to head back into the forest, a huge shadow flashed over us. Brad and I both looked up and saw the enormous, outstretched wings of a Golden Eagle not 20 feet above us. The eagle had jumped out from atop a tree on our left and was gliding out over the water to our right. The wingspan on these birds are massive, this one was at least six feet across. The brown feathers of the bird glowed amber as the sun shone through and it silently coasted away. It was a great experience of another animal encounter on the trail.

Once out of the lake's area we settled in for the endless sandy dirt roads ahead. Each mile ate our stamina and motivation through repetitive, sawtooth climbing. We began this detour chipper and thought we'd push through fairly quickly. But the heat! The desert! The trail morphed from straight, forested road with shade, to aimless and exposed curves through a burn area. It felt as if the road engineers themselves fell victim to the draining heat of the burnt hillsides. We zeroed in on a campground nearer to the halfway mark of the detour and metered our pace to try to ensure we'd arrive coherent. The sun failed to fall behind any cloud or mountain peak, and we were baking on the tan dirt road. Punching uphill switched to granny-gear, granny-gear switched to pushing our bikes. We were losing momentum and prayed that each corner we rounded, the campground would be there. We passed dozens of erratic bends to no relief. We were incredibly hot and I wasn't sure how much longer we'd last.

Near sunset, we began a shallow descent that aided in cooling our skin. As we swerved to match the winding road, we felt the temperature dropping around us. We plunged into a cool valley and the low vegetation perked from arid and crispy to lusher and greener. The dirt around us changed from dead tan to living grass. We rounded a corner that exposed tall pine trees in a valley and we could hear the rush of water. I crossed a bridge at good speed and started slowing to debate whether to fill our water bags while we could. And then I saw it.

The classic brown and pale-yellow sign of National Forest facilities. "Goose Creek Campground" was written above in brown letters. It was an oasis in the valley. The light was already well faded as we pulled in, totally exhausted. We were lucky enough to find an open campsite. We didn't have exact change for the site's fee. In fact, I only had twenty-dollar bills. I asked some other campers if they had change and our first assistance on the trail was sealed. Our neighbors helped break my twenty into ten's and although I still overpaid the drop box fee, it didn't hurt my feelings a bit. The water we heard was a solid stream about twenty feet wide and flowed right behind our tent area. We'd conquered the first half of the detour and could enjoy some relief. This campground even had vault toilets and real toilet paper. We filled our water bags and began rehydrating. Brad fired up his Jetboil and we cooked some instant meals supplemented by a few perishable items. The temperature plummeted quickly because the campground was crammed in a sharp valley. Not wanting it to get any colder, we took turns bathing in the river behind our tent. I don't think I'll ever forget the feeling of the sand, moss, and rocks under my feet as the frigid water cooled my legs until they were nearly numb. For whatever reason, I thoroughly enjoyed washing up at night and snuggling into my warm, dry, clean sleeping clothes. Before bed, we both finished some bike maintenance. We were making a habit of lubing the chain every day, and degreasing and lubing it every other or every third day. A quick wipe down of our suspension stanchions and we called it a night. I fell asleep to the white noise of the stream behind us.

I woke up in the morning to the same rush of water. The tent was still well dark, but we wanted to get up early to avoid the heat. But once again, my lack of efficient packing struck again. I needed to learn how to pack up faster in the morning. We woke up at 5am… and didn't leave until 6:45. This bag system has got to change! We did have a hot breakfast to help against the cold but that didn't account for all of the time I wasted. I was embarrassed. I was fumbling with bags and equipment and packing, forgetting, unpacking, repacking, etc. What a mess. Brad poked fun at me as his patience wore thin, and rightly so. I didn't realize I was behind until I looked over at Brad putting on his riding gloves. I still had most of my unorganized loot on the picnic table in camp. I hustled as fast as I could and promised myself I would never be that slow again for the rest of the trip.

We started off with determination to take on the rest of this desert. In the morning, without the heat, we were presented the gift of incredible and inspiring sunrise views on winding and open roads. We would climb a short distance and descend a short distance. Some of these downhills were longer sweeping descents at great speed! We smiled at each other and listened to the wind in our helmets as we leaned as hard as we dared on the dirt and gravel surface. We could see the road we were to follow in the distance, climbing out of the depression we were riding down into. That was ok for now, we were thrilled to be pacing off so much mileage before the heat hit.

But the heat did hit. It was delayed from our early start but we could tell our time was limited! We finished up the last of the sandy rolling hills as the heat increased. It quickly taxed our pace, water, and mental fortitude. After miles and miles of rolling our bikes through dirt, washboard bumps, and loose sand, we finally met the intersection with the paved Taryall Road. We were ecstatic. It was so smooth, so efficient, so effortless. Even the climbs were being accomplished above our third gear. Swift progress at last. It was time to turn and burn. We hooted up the first hill, admiring our good luck and pace, and crested the top. Rolling over the hill's peak, we immediately encountered strong headwinds as we traveled along this road southbound. Our good luck had been quickly snuffed and our pace diminished again. Brad tucked in behind me and we began switching places to take turns cutting the wind ahead and drafting each other to save energy. I remembered the shape of this detour in my mind and realized that soon we would turn northbound again and the headwind would reverse. I shared my thoughts with Brad and he agreed that it was reasonable, at least.

Big mistake. As we turned northbound, we found the wind was simply wrapping around the rising terrain to our right. It hugged the sloping hills in the same way we did along the road, only from the opposite direction. This was starting to hurt! We tucked down to make ourselves more aerodynamic and continued our aero-towing of each other along the pavement. I was laughing at the ridiculousness of the situation: Voluntarily out on a paved road, being passed by speeding cars, getting baked by the sun, head down and grinding against the wind, on aggressive mountain bikes full of gear. How did I get here!?

We finally reached a long downhill. This will be the longest paved downhill of the entire ride. The databook describes the road as passing through the "nearly abandoned town of Taryall". They were correct! At our rapid clip, I think we entered and exited the town in less than 30 seconds. We passed a historic, albeit boarded up early-century school house, a brand-new pre-fabricated steel fire station, and sporadic residences on large plots. That was it! Weeks ago, I thought perhaps there will be a place to purchase a snack at a gas station. No gas station, no shops, just a slight concentration of buildings and homes.

Our speed diminished as the descent reversed and we ground our way past ranches and other large fields. We administered a considerable effort against that stiff wind and eventually saw measurable progress to the end of the detour. Taryall Reservoir was the first landmark that indicated the end was closer. This was a huge body of water carved into the sandy and barren hills around us. It provided open panoramic views of cool, refreshing water lapping along the shoreline. We decided to stop and have lunch. I believe both of our lunches were cold. I ate some tuna out of a packet and slathered it onto a tortilla. I think I also remember a few slices of cheese and some honey and salt to supplement. Gourmet, I know. We'd already passed midday and we knew we ought to keep moving to make it to Kenosha Pass on time to greet our families. And so, we packed up again, took advantage of another real vault toilet, and rolled out of the small parking area and back onto the road.

A 360 degree view of the Reservoir and Taryall Road.

Our heads ducked under the wind again and we continued our formation riding along the road. We would be silent for twenty minutes, despite being only feet from each other, then we'd spend a few minutes to curse out the wind or a driver that passed too close. But each time we settled down and got back to grinding away the miles.

I had been keeping tabs on the end of the paved portion and knew we were closing in on it. As I looked as far up the road as I could see, hoping for evidence that this detour would end, I was distracted by a confusing sign passing on my left. I glanced first, and my eyes returned to the road. But my brain processed what the sign actually said and I looked again. *Stagestop Store & Saloon*? Brad saw it about the same time and yelled to me, "Is this a mirage??". We shrugged and decided it was worth investigating. Sure as shootin', in a big red barn-like building, a gruff but helpful guy sold us a few energy bars, bags of chips and two ice-cold Cokes. Just because they don't smile doesn't mean they don't care about you! We chatted about the racers that come through each year and he gave us some information about the area. He pointed us to a spigot on the side of his store that we could fill up with clean water. We were plenty grateful and stepped outside to do just that. We finished our snacks and first "Victory Cokes" of the ride, chucked the cans, and rejoined the road. Not a half-mile up the hill, we turned right off the road and rolled over dirt once again.

We could tell the pavement trend was reversing. It deteriorated (well...depending on who you ask) from asphalt to dirt road, then to dirt double track, and finally we saw our old friend the singletrack. After a few miles of climbing and improving views, our success was confirmed and a small sign said *Colorado Trail No. 1776.* What a total b----- of a reroute.

Intercepting the CT again after that immense detour felt fantastic. We pedaled up the remaining climb into an area that began to look familiar. Every fall we hike around here to explore the exploding yellow and orange aspen trees. I cannot describe the color of these intense forests at their peak of turning. I implore you to find a quiet corner of the mountain for yourself some September. You will not be disappointed.

We reached the high point of this very short stint on the end of Segment 5 (we skipped Segment 4 thanks to the detour) and looked down onto Kenosha Pass below. The day's work was done and Brad and I got pumped up before we blasted into the trail below. Descending through the Kenosha Aspens into camp was an absolute grin. It was a section of spontaneous smiling. The trail started more open with thin patches of aspens punctuating our surroundings saturated with grass. It was skinny and rocky but flowing well. Eventually, the forest packed in tight but the trail widened into an absolute bomb of a descent. I was having the ride of my life. I'd ridden here before but, geezus, it never felt like this! The trail was wide enough to get playful with small line selections. Brad might dart left around an obstacle and I'd pop off it. He'd take a drop and I'd swerve on the berm instead. We were flying. The woods erupted with our yelling and screaming. I imagined Brad and I taking some turns on skis here in the winter. What an idea! We finished the fantastic descent and emerged in the lower camp area.

The aspen lined descent to Kenosha Pass. Imagine this in the fall in bright orange!

We both were looking forward to seeing the ladies tonight and eating a real meal. We crossed highway 285 that travels through the pass and continued into the campground on the other side. As we traveled around the various campsites, we finally found the post with Brad's name on it. In a few hours, our families would reunite and we'd spend a night camping here at exactly 10,000 feet. That night we told stories of our experience so far. We laughed at and animated the crazy events we'd gone through in only 120 miles. Two of our other great friends, Lisi and Maria, joined us at the site too. True to form, they helped me finish the whiskey I had hidden away in my bag. Lord knows I didn't want to carry it anymore and any intention or desire of getting drunk had vaporized. Elissa whistled at Brad while he took a camp shower, and I pulled Jordan close to me and we enjoyed the campfire. I love these friends and this was a great night of the usual unorganized mild chaos. We pounded some food and got a good night's sleep. I snuggled close to Jordan that night and greatly appreciated the extra layers of blankets she brought and the warmth and comfort of her body in my arms. It's just...not the same with Brad.

This Trail is Amazing!
(Segments 6-8, The "Break"enridge Layover, and some Classic Favorites)

The next day we'd made the decision to make the best of this upcoming section. While Elissa cooked breakfast, Brad and I stripped our bikes of our bags. Jordan, Elissa, and Kennedy were going to meet us in Breckenridge that evening and we let the car carry our gear into Breckenridge. This would leave us free of weight and free to slash down the hill. This too was another section that we've both ridden before (once together, even) and we were looking forward to this run. The planning was minimal and we blasted off after helping clean up camp a little.

Just leaving Kenosha Pass and descending into Jefferson Valley

This segment begins in more of the gorgeous aspen tree patches common to this area. You spend much of your time in the beginning navigating some short punchy climbs over some of the thicker roots we have out in Colorado. Occasionally, we were rewarded with huge views into the wide and flat valley of Jefferson's ranches. After the first few punches, we settled in for a long gradual climb to Georgia Pass. The pass's saddle reaches 11,874 feet in elevation and we spent a few hours to achieve it. This first half of the ride is more commonly ridden. It's easier, logistically, to ride the twelve miles to the saddle and then return on the same trail back to Kenosha Pass than it is to arrange a shuttle for pickup in Breckenridge. We were excited to push over the top and get into the lesser ridden areas.

At the top of Georgia Pass

The trail leaving Georgia Pass was long, somewhat steep, and fairly consistent descent deep into the thicker forests below. Equally consistent was the endless rock gardens that demanded huge amounts of full-body strength and agility to stay on the bike! This area is one of those sections that is not overly difficult if taken slow, but requires a huge amount of skill to add any speed at all. Our forearms burned from our grip on the bars, and we were winded even while we weren't pedaling. This section gets so deep into the forest that the trail becomes lusher and there are many spots that have a trickle of water passing through the rocks and over the trail itself. It's a great adrenaline rush to finish this section in one piece, but you do pay a toll on your endurance! I'm very happy we didn't give up our full-suspension bikes for a hardtail model. Having some give in the rear end was priceless.

I was feeling some major fatigue in my upper body after the descent and I didn't get much rest before my lower body was again needed. We soon started a steep climb out of the bottom of the profile. We again climbed about 1,500 feet in only three miles or so. We knew this climb was coming and tried hard to push through it. Once you reach the top, the work is over and it's a long chunky but flowing descent into Breckenridge. We cranked out the elevation required in this final climb although I don't remember much from this section.

Once on top of our final climb, we caught our breath with a snack. The long descending trail ahead was in fact so long, that it would also tax our bodies before we were out of the wilderness. We packed up and pushed on to find the first parts of the descending slopes. This section of downhill has much more flow and less "gnar" than the early descent we undertook. The rock gardens are far fewer, shorter, and didn't include any bar-flipping obstacles like before. Our speed was generally great and we whooped and hollered over some of the more exciting bits. As we got closer to town, we could start seeing structures peek out of the woods ahead. My arms were starting to cramp occasionally and my lower back burned from the constant attacking position I held over my bike. We cleaned up that last few high-speed straights between switchbacks before we ended in a mountain neighborhood below.

I was gassed. I'd hit the trail hard that day and overspent what I had in the bank. We got to the running path next to the main road to Breckenridge and split away from the CT, southbound. It didn't take long for us to give in to the lumbering Breck Shuttle and catch a ride into town. We racked our bikes and boarded the nearly full bus (I was self-conscious about how bad I stunk, sorry folks) and tried to pick the best location for drop off. I was fading fast and just wanted to be in a bed with food in my belly. We departed the bus in the middle of downtown Breckenridge and set off to find our hotel.

As soon as I arrived, my health took a surprising nose-dive. The first sign of trouble was my mental acuity. I was far off my usual game. I had already forgotten my sunglasses on the bus and when we arrived at the hotel, I couldn't sort out which of the hotel's buildings our room was in. Brad noticed my mental state immediately and even our wives knew I was in trouble when I walked through the door. I'm still not sure what it was in the end. Moderate nausea, no desire to eat or drink, I had to force feed myself dinner, constipated, and bad chills. Dehydration and constipation, perhaps. Maybe food poisoning. Add in a total change of diet combined with immense physical effort and my body boarded the Nope-Train headed for Not-Todayville. I sat in a vegetative state on the couch for quite a while before I could muster some signs of life again. I again have to thank Jordan for her significant help with this too. She went to the store with me and helped choose items to aid my recovery. Together, we found some electrolyte drinks, fruits, some diet and vitamin supplement I know nothing about, and even one of those tourist oxygen cans--just to rule out altitude sickness. Later that evening, I tried to enjoy a dip in the hot tub with the group but was mostly just uncomfortable. As the evening progressed, I was starting to feel better but it was still coming in waves. Jordan and I even meditated together in a quiet corner of the hotel. Eventually, we went to bed without being able to enjoy what was supposed to be a fun overnight out with our families. Jordan really suffered because she was looking forward to our stay together. All night I was hit with waves of chills, was stuck in the fetal position, and enjoyed only intermittent restless sleep. I was in serious doubt about my recovery and how things will go. All the while, I intensely regretted not being able to spend better time with Jordan. She sacrificed so much for me to accomplish this ride and this night was supposed to be more reuniting and less nursing a lifeless husband.

Dawn spread across the dark horizon I'd been staring at all night and I rose feeling better but not anywhere near 100%. The ladies prepared breakfast for the whole group in the kitchenette of our hotel room. I ate breakfast quietly, rather unsure of my actual situation. Eventually, I ran out of time to stall any longer and, despite my doubts and fear, decided to put my nuts back into my riding shorts and give it a go anyway. We both dumped a load of useless items. It was embarrassing some of the things we thought we would have the time for. Cameras and mounts, fishing gear, bracelet weaving, night riding, reading, etc. My goal was to completely eliminate my secondary "Quasi" pack and did so. We packed the rest of our bare essentials into our new, more efficient configurations. I said goodbye, sad and regretful, and feeling like garbage. But I can't quit now, I'd never forgive myself.

We glided out of the hotel with our chin straps undone and gloves in our back pockets. The first stint today was only to the bus stop. We waited in the sunshine at the BreckConnect Gondola station and caught the bus back to where we left the trail at Gold Camp road. We had talked about this upcoming section last night. It was a doozy, 3700 feet of climbing in 13 miles. Fingers crossed I don't puke, pass out, or shit myself in the first 3 miles. Once we arrived, we pedaled into immediate and intense first gear climbing and pushing on rough, recently deforested trail. For an encore, this was followed by baby-head sized rocks on "mining roads". Try riding a bike on an uphill trail of loose softballs, only sharper. Lesson learned: Miner's make the worst roads. Always. I have no idea how they moved turn of the century equipment over such bad terrain.

An example of a steep pitch of trail near Gold Camp

Then it happened. The first breakdown of the trail. I had stopped during this climb to add some electrolyte powder to my Camelback reservoir. I was packing everything back into my downtube bag when the zipper's two halves separated on the wrong side of the sliding mechanism. "MOTHER#@$%^#", I yelled aloud. I don't know why, but zipper blowouts have always been particularly demoralizing for me (does anyone else feel that way?). The soft metal of the cheap zipping device flexed far enough to allow the two halves of teeth material to slip out. Cooked. I tried to my best abilities to repair the zipper, but couldn't get the teeth to join in their original format. Without that strength, another blowout was inevitable and I decided the bag must go under the knife. Temporarily held shut with a few safety pins, I caught up to Brad. We took the time to "stitch" the bag two-thirds of the way shut with a few puncture holes and zip ties. This allowed me to continue to store my repair gear and water in the bag, accessible from the top. The repair held well as the bag material is actually quite sturdy. We didn't yet realize it would be a battle with these cheap zippers for the rest of the trip.

My frame bag with blown zipper. Zip ties used to hold part of the seam.

Underway again, and riding gingerly at first to test the repair, we wound our way through the forest over miles of very rough climbing. After a few hours of the baby-heads, we finally broke the tree line for the first real alpine views of the trail so far. This was the huge boost we needed to complete this difficult day. I felt some improvement in myself and was gaining confidence that I could get back on track. It was great to see us getting closer to the bare peaks above us. This was the real deal of what the trail is known for.

I'm going to digress for a moment to bring up something I said earlier. At the end of segment 3, I mentioned that our pace was "...drifting from **the schedule**...". I used that word with intention because of the lesson we learned at this very moment. I brought up the feeling and Brad furthered the thought. The outdoors educated us on how futile keeping a schedule on the trail was. Unfortunately, we had been forced into an intense push of effort to meet with our family at Kenosha Pass and Breckenridge. That deadline heaped pressure onto the ride that wasn't conducive to enjoyment. After the meetup, we had no deadlines at all, just an end goal. The closest thing to a deadline was Brad's requirement to get back to his work before his vacation days ran out. Even that had some leniency. So, when we encountered our first equipment failure, I think at first I was in a rush to finish the repair and then hustle up trail to recover the time. After we started pedaling again, a wave of relief passed over me with our discussion. Phrases like, "We've got to get 13 more miles in before the sun goes down" were replaced by "Yeah dude, we'll stop when we get tired or the sun goes down". This changed the dynamic of the rest of the trip. The smile returned.

Entering the alpine zone after Breckenridge

Ahead of us was tough sections of steep pushing, but the views! It's getting real! We were still in familiar stomping grounds, but the experience was changing. Prior to this, the trail was very recognizable from our previous rides and only a bit of it really took us into tree line alpine riding. Now we've climbed one of the highest elevation gains in a single section, well above the tree line, and we did ok in the process. It's our first window into new trail and what the CT holds ahead. We rode up and over the ridge of the numbered peaks behind Breckenridge Resort and onto a grassy mountainside with a wide-open view of Copper Mountain Resort on the other side.

Alpine trail between Breckenridge and Copper Mountain Resorts. You can see the ski runs at Copper.

We descended on the other side first on tricky and steep trail cut into a steep mountainside. We wore quite a bit of pad material off our brakes over these few miles. This eventually let down into the forest on fast and flowing downhill trail that was a joy to run at full speed. The whole area was marked with a few recently avalanched sections of total forest destruction. The amount of carnage was incredible and there was still moving snow and ice underfoot as we walked through. After our ride, I saw a few pictures on social media of sinkholes opening up where the snow melted away. Sketchy stuff! This segment was the first big test of the trail and it was tough but we did it, and we felt positive about it all too! We enjoyed a sandwich and coke and did a little chain maintenance at the gas station at the bottom of the descent. I felt like I was back in action. Refueled, we pointed west once again toward Copper Mountain and Segment 8.

A 360 degree view of the carnage of the avalanched area

Segment 8. Be still, my heart. This is a personal favorite of both Brad and I. We've ridden this segment before as part of the "Dirty Copper Triangle". The first part of this trail winds through the resort and crosses over many of the dry ski runs at Copper Mountain. It eventually leaves the resort boundary and works up the edge of a long and shallow valley. This area had two avalanched sections that appeared pretty fresh. One even seemed to show an avalanche that began *in the trees* of the dense forest. It didn't show the typical avalanche evidence we'd seen before, where the slide begins in the high mountains and slams into the forest below. This slide had intact and untouched forest *above the slide* with carved out trees below. Very strange, we didn't know that could happen! Our favorite section of the day was climbing past Janet's Cabin and up and over Searle Pass, all the way to Kokomo Pass and the following descent. It's wonderful trail in gorgeous alpine scenery and we did it all at sunset and into dusk. I will never forget riding this section with Brad and descending into camp that night. It seems rare in these modern times to have so much fun that you can't stop smiling, even after you're lying in your sleeping bag.

This section delivered. We descended hurriedly from Kokomo Pass with rapidly fading light, searching for a reasonable place for a tent. This came quite a bit later, as we passed a few tents of others already in the sack. We found camp 3 miles and 700ft above Camp Hale at Cataract Creek, nearly at dark.

Views from Searle and Kokomo Passes and the sunset descent into camp

This camp was a pleasantly lush and forested site with plenty of space and a rock fire ring with logs to sit. Not that we have any time for a fire! It reminded me more of the Pacific Northwest than it did Colorado. We ate the second half of our gas station sammies and started bed chores. I walked through the dark, barefoot on the mossy ground, toward the sound of rushing water. I continued our night time ritual and took another naked and abbreviated bath in the cascading creek of crisp, clear, but freezing current. I'm dead serious, there is something about washing up with nothing but a headlamp on, and operating alone in a single cone of red light in the otherwise total darkness of nature. It's a unique memory and feeling I will cherish! Try it sometime.

We finished that day without accomplishing major mileage, but instead conquered an enormous chunk of elevation, and both slept like rocks accordingly.

Something New on Something Old
(Segment 8 and 9.5)

Next to tackle was a short descent into the historic Camp Hale site. We woke up early again to 40-degree temperatures and frost. This was our first cold morning of perhaps a half-dozen to come. We broke camp quickly (after we ditched the numerous items in Breckenridge, I had since gotten my act together and nailed down a faster camp routine) and had a minimal breakfast. We expected to make Leadville in short time and would enjoy a large stack of pancakes in town. Naturally, our estimates were largely erroneous.

Descending from our campsite and into Camp Hale was a fun, rough and rowdy singletrack that gave way to double track nearer to the bottom. We shouted at the trail and the bitter cold wind. I figured the sun would warm the area so fast I didn't don my cold gear. I was freezing. My fingers and toes went numb and I regretted not having doubled-down on my layers. Living in the valley of Camp Hale must have been dreadfully biting in the wintertime.

As we leveled out at the valley bottom, we cruised along a dirt road that lined the former grounds of the Camp Hale historic site. We ended up missing our first turn due to an absent trail marker and, unaware, continued along a tour of the grounds. I noticed we'd been heading north through the valley floor for a while instead of the expected west. After consulting the maps, were indeed in the wrong place.

Crossing the floor of the Pando Valley and former Camp Hale

For me, this was a blessing in disguise. I had wanted to see these grounds for a long time because the site has a lot of meaning to Colorado and even some of my friends. Camp Hale is the former training ground of the famed 10th Mountain Division of the US Army. The 10th was formed during World War II to accomplish the unique and unfamiliar task of fighting effectively in the mountains of Italy, Austria, and other alpine theaters. They picked professionals, experts, and hobbyists of all types of alpine activity such as Nordic skiing, homesteading, and mountaineering and survival and began to train in that very valley. The valley was considered a close representation of the working environment in the combat zones in Europe. At one point, the camp, now totally abandoned and almost fully reclaimed, housed more than 15,000 personnel and had main and cross streets! Evidence of the camp still clearly remains. There are some dilapidated concrete bunker frames in the northern half of the valley, and we passed immediately adjacent to some earth-topped concrete ammunition bunkers and a few subtle training foxholes during our ride. In the area of the site, camping and off-trail travel is prohibited due to the chance of encountering *unexploded ordnance!* The area was used for many years before eventually being broken down. Members of the 10th are said to have loved the area so much that some returned to open some of the now-famous ski resorts, including Vail and Ski Cooper. Other reminders include the 10th Mountain Hut System (huts.org), a large monument at Ski Cooper Resort, and Nordic trails and tree markings in early segment 9. Once used for overland training by the 10th, volunteers and private owners now maintain the system as reservable hut and yurt accommodations for backcountry skiers and backpackers. If you ever see a vintage picture or statue of a white-camouflaged soldier on or with skis, that's the 10th Mountain OG's. What's cool, personally, is many of my military friends from college are now or were helicopter pilots in varying sub-branches of the modern-day 10th, now based in Fort Drum, NY. Camp Hale is in the Pando Valley, and they nicknamed themselves the *Pando Commandos.* The mascot at the time was a Panda bear descending on skis with a rifle.

Camping not allowed in the area due to the possibility of unexploded ordnance

Old munitions bunkers in Camp Hale

Winter soldiers training in Camp Hale, the "Pando Commandos"; and a view of the former Camp

After realizing our error, we doubled-back on the road and found a CT volunteer crew now working to install the very marker that was missing when we passed the intersection! Talk about service! We continued out of the picturesque Swiss-like open valley and into the woods. After paralleling US Highway 24 on rolling and rocky singletrack, we eventually crossed the highway and hopped a set of railroad tracks. We meandered through another gorgeous open meadow and found our way to an abandoned railbed. The smooth, train-qualified grade of the old line provided a pleasant pedal to the finish of segment 8. At the end of segment 8 were Ski Cooper ski area, some ruins of old coking ovens, the 10th Mountain Division memorial, and Tennessee Pass trailhead.

We continued on after a short break at the trailhead bathrooms and wound through a pine forest of well-kept trail marked with frequent multi-use signs of many colors. We realized these trails were used for more than biking as some of the signs were installed high on the trees --- in case the snowfall was deep enough to cover a normally installed sign! These trails are shared with Nordic skiers and snowshoers in the winter season and the some of the huts in the 10th Mountain system are nearby. Many of the tree's markings are physical cuts from the early, less arbor-conscious days of blazing trail. Harsh, but effective, and they've stood the test of time. Looking at the age of the healing wounds I suspect they may even stretch all the way to the training days of the 10th Mountain soldiers doing what they do best.

A Holy Oasis
(Holy Cross/Mt. Massive Detour through Leadville)

Brad on the pavement of the Holy Cross Detour, set to a gorgeous mountain backdrop

The trail joined with a dirt road that passed through the forest maze of singletrack intersections. This was the beginning of the next required 22-mile detour for us bikers. We descended on this wide and well-graded gift to a neighborhood, onto paved streets, and eventually onto US Highway 24. We shared the road successfully with numerous passing vehicles until this long, high-speed pedal brought us alongside a great view of the nearby Collegiate Peaks to our west. We glided into Leadville without too much effort. After snagging a fresh peach and some restaurant advice from a woman running a local fruit stand, we cruised into main street like weathered cowboys after a cattle drive. The bustling commotion of tourists and traffic and historic buildings was almost sensory overload! We made it! We smiled, gazing around, and I savored our success. The woman at the stand led us to Tennessee Pass Cafe, and it did not disappoint. In fact, I'd consider that nugget of information as the second small piece of Trail Magic that we received. We spread our gear on a patio table and both smashed a huge meal that satisfied our bodies and minds into blissful content. Any doubts about my appetite and previous ailments were washed away after this meal. We both tacked on a few refills of Coke during 20 minutes of relaxing and were out the door and back at it. We rode out of that wonderful oasis and back onto the open road. The treats were not over yet.

Our arrival into Leadville and lunch at the Tennessee Pass Cafe

The Wild and Glorious Descent into Twin Lakes
(Segment 11)

After leaving the pavement again, we spent a good deal of time grinding out a slow climb on graded dirt roads through standard Colorado pine forest. The area was lonely even as we passed a few empty campgrounds and rejoined the trail. Some parts of the trail make you feel like civilization abandoned the area. It's a different feeling from the isolation of the backcountry. Once humans had made a life and often visited here, for example, but something has changed to cause them to leave. It's closer to, "...Why *isn't* anyone camping here right now?" and makes you wonder what they know that you don't.

Brad's bike pointed back into the mountains after leaving Leadville, still on the detour

But like so many other potentially morbid questions to come, we ignored it and moved forward! We rejoined the trail at the Mt. Massive trailhead, the start of segment 11. This section began with 5 miles of singletrack through a number of pine and aspen forests lingering around 10,500 feet. At the 5-mile mark, the trail transitioned into a steady, perfect, brake-free downhill grade of fantastic shape and lined with aspen trees. Many times, already, we've been disappointed by looking forward to a descending grade only for it to end up lacking rideability or length. This was not the case in segment 11. The cautious optimism grew to euphoria. This descent was simply beautiful. So beautiful in fact, that we weren't the only ones enjoying the forest!

As we descended into the forest, Brad followed my lead, riding about 100 feet behind. We were cruising pedal-free through long curves as the aspens whipped past. As we rounded a long left-handed bend, I was startled out of my tunneled focus by an enormous commotion to my left, just inside the trees. It sounded like boulders were falling through the forest! While stopping as best I could, I tried to spot what was happening but was still moving too fast to make any sense of the extremely brief glances I could afford. Only when I was nearly stopped did I not only make sense but actually made eye contact with two local natives! A large, assumingly female black bear with amber tinged fur, and her adolescent cub were losing their shit in the woods not more than 50 feet from me. It was a case of mutual surprise.

I turned back up the trail and yelled to Brad, "BEARS! BEARS! BEARS!". But the cub had already had enough, immediately panicked, and tore off up the trail *toward*

Brad! Brad later commented that he heard my yelling but couldn't make out what I'd said. Only when he was playing chicken with the cub did he realize, *Ohhh, 'BEARS!'*. Seeing Brad coming down the trail, the cub darted off the path and uphill to Brad's right. This inconveniently put both Brad and I between Mom and her kiddo and placed us into the worst-case category you've only ever read about. Mama bear began snorting and growling and pacing back and forth. She stood up and down from her hind legs repeatedly and made more eye contact with me, searching desperately for her offspring.

I remembered learning that a bear standing isn't necessarily a sign of threat, the bear is simply trying to get a better vantage point to figure out, "just what the f--- is going on here?!". However, this was also about the moment that my head filled with serious, honest doubt about how this was going to turn out. I assumed, in the next moment, this bear would take off toward me and attack, defending her cub, and all I could do is try to keep my bike between myself and her. The distance was so close, it wouldn't have mattered if I had a rocket-launcher, she'd be tearing me up before I could get anything out. I didn't know if I was already inside her minimum-response-radius, having ridden right over the 'line in the sand'. I figured I was and truly felt my life was in a good chance of serious danger. I believed, this being the worst-case scenario, the attack was already assured. My heart quickly sank to a realization that this might be it, I was out of control now, and how stupid it would be. These were my real emotions at the time, eye to eye with the bear. I sadly thought, *Oh no*. The bear felt intensely close and I alone and woefully unprepared in that moment. I actually remember hoping Brad didn't come down the trail to help so only one of us would get shredded.

Brad yelled down to me, "Do you see the mama bear?!" to which I fervently responded to the affirmative. Currently, mama bear was about 40 or so feet away in the woods to my 8 o'clock, left and slightly behind, and mean-muggin' me. Some more yelling occurred, we were quickly debating what action to take, but I honestly don't remember what was said. My memory picks up again at thinking I need to *stop yelling*. I calmed my responses down and Brad concluded I should continue down the trail, he'd back up the trail, and we'd separate for a few minutes. That would let mom cross the trail and go find her damned runner, and we'd rejoin. I remember being worried about separating in this situation, but I was already beyond mama slightly and trusted his cooler judgment of the problem. In hindsight, if Brad came rolling down the trail toward mom, things could have easily gotten worse. I trusted and agreed and we followed the plan. I slowly rolled away on my bike and then picked up speed. After ten or so seconds of riding (as if I could even estimate time in that moment), I waited down the trail a hundred yards.

A long time passed. I sat on my bike, looking over my shoulder, ready to bolt if a blob of brown fur was coming down the trail.

True to form, Brad soon rolled in casually with a big smile on his face, cool as a cucumber.

Brad coming down the trail to rejoin me after the encounter, still intact and smiling.

I remember the actions of the bears being surprisingly human. Maybe our actions are really just animalistic. The kid freaked and ran off like a child getting loose from her mom and running toward and across the street. Before she could even react to corral the toddler, he was already crossing lanes! The mom couldn't do anything but fear and hope for her kid in total dread as she watched the cars go by between her and her child. That's exactly how it felt, honestly, the reactions and body language were identical. Once the cub had crossed the trail and was well away from us, the mood changed. Mom was looking at Brad and I, now more suspicious than fearful. In hindsight, I sensed less desperation ("Don't touch my child!"), and instead more posturing ("We're not going to have a f-ing problem, right?"). Bizarre and fascinating to look back on.

Sadly, it happened too fast and was too intense to have the presence of mind to turn a camera on.

Brad and I spoke about the whole ordeal for a few minutes while I was coming off the adrenaline dump and endorphin rush. We compared what we saw and how wild the encounter had been. I did roll the camera for this part, and you can hear, embarrassingly, how I'm still at level-10 and highly animated during the conversation. We turned downhill again and resumed our blissful descent, skin and adventure intact.

The sun was low, the sky scattered with clouds, and the light coming through the trees. Brad commented that the temperature, the wind, the light, the effortless speed, the packed dirt and mild rocks of the trail, absolutely everything was so right. After our bear encounter, it made for a stress-free, involuntarily grinning, teary-eyed, blast of a descent. We broke out of the woods at high speed and the sight of Twin Lakes before us was jaw-dropping. Two pristine lakes, well below, nestled into an immense valley with the sun peeking behind the mountains and spreading Lion-King-grade beams of light across the waters. We slashed and swerved our way down the flowing trail, screaming, laughing, and cheering. I never wanted it to end. It was beautiful, emotional, and deeply satisfying. It's an experience I will treasure.

The view during our descent into Twin Lakes

The first of the Twin Lakes, just as our descent finished and our circumventing of the lakes began

We reached the bottom of the descent to open and wandering singletrack that followed the shoreline of the lakes. The trail rounded the lake opposite the sunset and the sight was enormous. We crossed the lakes' outflow dam and took in the view while coming off the high of the descent. I wish I could share the sight in-person with all of you.

The dam marked the lowest elevation of segment 11 and we had a decision to make. I preferred to push on. The hour was still somewhat early, about 5 pm, and I still had the urge (albeit dying urge) to put in 5 more miles every night. Brad preferred to call it a day due to the perfection of our would-be campsite. When he spelled out a long recovery break, an open and level campground with water, a bigger dinner, and even a swim, I was convinced. Brad was doing a good job of driving our decisions today and so I trusted that man and was happy I did. It was good to take an evening off and in a wonderful location.

We walked around the lake area and saw plenty of fire rings and camp evidence but we simply didn't know the rules of the area. Was this a campground? There were no signs. Do we pay someone a fee? There were no facilities or personnel. Other campers (owners of a glorious 5th-wheel, gooseneck camper) strolled by and so we asked. They replied, "Oh this is BLM land. You can camp wherever you like and it's free. Taxes and stuff, you know?". We had no idea we'd made it to Bureau of Land Management areas. In fact, we didn't know who's land we'd be on since we left Waterton Canyon. We chatted with them for a few minutes and found the middle-aged couple work remotely via satellite internet. He winked, "We'll enjoy about another month of these sunsets before we find another BLM spot just as nice... pretty loose schedule". Damn, just imagine!

I was able to catch enough service from the nearby village to make a phone call home to Jordan. I gave her an update on our progress and condition and caught up with her life for a bit. As the evening grew darker and dinner and chores complete, I finally had the time to reflect on our progress and experiences, looking weathered but Instagram-worthy at the lake's edge. I took a few sunset photos, tossed off my clothes, and jumped in the lake. Like one does. We cleaned up 50 miles that day and cheated death. We were only 9 miles behind the original 11-day plan! I was exhilarated on our recent progress. It was the conclusion to an excellent evening in every sense of the word, and we settled in for our first night of 8+ hours of sleep.

A Fork in the Road, the Mythical Milestone
(Segment 11)

Dawn at our Twin Lakes camp

Twilight blued the night sky and we arose to 41 Degrees of biting cold. Despite the shivers, we woke up just before dawn and enjoyed a beautiful sunrise and took some amazing pictures. Brad and I enjoyed the deep purple light over a small breakfast and instant coffee, trying to warm up. I was treated to the most scenic coffee poop that I've had all trip, maybe the best in my life. Fantastic.

We again planned to have a bigger meal in the next resupply town of Buena Vista so our breakfast was thin. I'm sure you can guess how that decision is going to go. We packed up from our best campsite of the trip so far and pedaled away. Back on the trail we rode a fantastic rim tour of the glassy lake itself. Flat, fast and fun. This section was reminiscent of West Branch Lake in Ohio, where I grew up boating with my family and friends. The similarity made me smile as we warmed up for the days push. It was goodbye to the morning's incredible light, spread between gorgeous trees, and the twin lakes to our right.

The trail marker indicating the beginning of the Collegiate East-West split

In short time we came to a simple, vertical trail marker. It indicated that if we continued straight on the trail, we'd find ourselves on the Collegiate West section of trail. Turning left, we'd follow the Collegiate East section, the original Colorado Trail. I remember staring and smiling at the sign. I had used this split as a planning benchmark for many months prior to the ride. It was surreal to be standing at the exact point that was so recognizable on the maps of the CT. It had no royal arch saying, "Collegiate West Entrance", or any other fancy designation. I suspect its importance is totally missed by most uneducated dayhikers.

This simple decision of the two directions creates a massive split in the trail, over 70 miles in length and more than 12 miles wide in one place. I looked in the direction of the newer Collegiate West trail longingly. Remember, riders cannot take the West section because of its passage through Wilderness Areas. Reports and reviews fabled the section as including some of the most amazing views and intimate mountain trails. Someday I'll return and experience the treasures of this forbidden section on foot.

After passing the sign, we began the Collegiate East route. We switchbacked up and over the valley wall and away from the great views of the Twin Lakes scenery. Some of these sections were quite steep and unrideable. We were on and off the bikes at regular intervals. I surprised myself thinking back to this section and initially not remembering it being so bad. When I referenced my trail journal, it corrected my memory, "...from there the trail is extremely steep and hot. A miserable push. I'm proud Brad and I boosted each other to finish the climb. The top was not satisfying, nor was the *descent. These local builders need to take some advice from the pros"*. Yeesh, salty-Matt rearing his head! Once I read my notes, I quickly recalled the extensive pushing that morning. To add insult to injury, at some point near this point in our trail progress, Brad's large water filtering bag had sprung a pinhole leak. The leak could be stopped simply by pressing on it with a finger. However, this didn't make filtering water very easy, and storing water in the bag resulted in a swamping the rest of his gear. We were forced to deal with this leak for the remainder of the ride.

On the opposite end of this climb was a numerous set of switchbacks down to a steep mountainside. This zigged and zagged us down this valley wall until we reached the bottom floor and dirt road of the next detour. This descent was fun and rather well built in comparison to the previous climb to get there. The terrain was covered in low scrub brush and therefore provided a wide open view of the entire area. We enjoyed this plunge to the bottom. It provided us with a much needed rest before we began our next many miles on the roads below.

The views of the final descent of Segment 11

Buena Vista, True to the Translation
(Collegiate Peaks Wilderness Detour)

Nine miles of trail since the lakes, crossing and following various forest and mining roads (remember what I said about miners and their roads?), and we had reached the next required detour routing us through Buena Vista. The 28-mile Collegiate Peaks Wilderness detour began with a smooth and paved road with a following grade. We made good time knocking off these first miles, taking a breather from the effort of the singletrack of Segment 11. Nine miles in, you cross the Arkansas River and the detour regains its rustic roots. From here, the detour follows an old railbed of the Colorado Midland Railroad. We were again biking through history along the stagecoach and rail route of mining and passenger travel days long ago. The scenery and sound of the river canyon were refreshing. The railbed even passed through a few old tunnels where routing the tracks around the rocks was apparently more difficult than just blasting a hole through them. This was a neat surprise and we took some fun pictures. I hollered like a train whistle as I passed under the deep archways. After nine more miles of this dirt road we again crossed the river and rolled into downtown BV.

Leaving Segment 11 behind us, we start on the Collegiate Peaks Detour

Passing through the old railroad tunnels along the Arkansas River

Buena Vista feels much more decentralized than Leadville, and the original historic downtown is small and almost required searching out for. In town, we took turns guarding the bikes while we resupplied at a grocery store. I picked up two donuts that can be found at almost every grocery store and gas station. Why not, right? I'm crushing calories, right? We stopped at a local Mexican joint that was kind enough to let us charge our electronics (trail magic!) while we destroyed limb-sized burritos. We ate as much as we dared in preparation for our next long haul. This was our last major stop before our longest stint in the backcountry. We had one top-off box waiting for us at a campground ahead, but after that, multiple days were required before our next proper stop in Silverton. We saddled up our fully-laden frames and rolled back into the heat, westbound toward Segment 13.

We passed multiple charming Colorado-ranch style residences on fairly large properties as we left BV. The area was lusher than I expected, taking advantage of the plentiful irrigation from the river I suppose. That didn't stop the heat, however, and as we got further from town the farmlands became more arid and desolate. We passed a seriously-vintage drive-in theater called, *The Commanche*. Opened in 1966, it looked righteously worn and weathered, like a film set from *Breaking Bad*. I deeply want to return and watch something backdropped by the mountain views and night sky. This time with a full cooler of beer and ice. And maybe in September. I bet the lot doesn't hold more than 50 cars and the screen has seen its fair share of black and white. We continued past and cleaned up the 10 miles of road of increasing grade until it wore us into extremely hot hiking on pavement. The road snaked into the mountains and we crisscrossed the centerline just for the shade. We climbed the road to the Avalanche Trailhead, aptly named for the visible carnage in the valley of past snow seasons. Here we rejoin the CT partway through Segment 13.

The Commanche drive-in theater

Oasis before the Sufferfest
(Segment 13)

Trail after Avalanche Trailhead was a very rocky, poorly optimized section for bikers. It certainly passed through areas of avalanche activity which could clearly be seen in the valley. That also meant the trail passed through areas with steep walls held together by endless rock features. This made for more pushing, crawling, and loss of time. The hike-a-bike was still incredibly hot, but being back in this relatively lush forest added humidity to the formula as well. We climbed hard on switchbacks up and eventually over a saddle near Bald Mountain. The trail crossed a few creeks and streams, and we found ourselves at the top of the elevation profile near mile fourteen.

Finishing off the end of the detour and preparing to join the CT again further up the hill. Note the avalanche runs on the valley walls, left of the road

We came out of the woods and followed the wild, Dr.-Seuss-wavy, 4x4 Mt. Princeton road down into an immensely open valley. The rain had carved a deep wandering channel into the middle of the road, and both sides of the channel, where vehicle tires would go, varied in height like competing roller coasters. We played on these huge, bizarre ribbons of bacon-shaped dirt, jumping and crossing from one side to the other while bombing downhill to civilization below. These features boosted our spirits and made us realize we were out of the worst of the day. It was another huge accomplishment. We yelled and cheered as we jumped as high as we dared with our laden bikes. The wind in our face, cooling us from the long arduous climb out of Buena Vista, was a heavenly feeling. We soon passed out of the dirt road and onto pavement. We left a few iconic Colorado ranches behind us and arrived quite suddenly at Mt. Princeton Hot Springs.

This small resort today includes three pools, a few hotel and cottage buildings, and some small places to eat and entertain. It's a relatively simple resort but has been renovated many times and is rather upscale and modern

for the area. This resort has a long history though, and you can see many of those touches still. It was established in 1879 and expanded slowly since. Straddling over Chalk Creek are the most historic buildings. Made of sandstone or something similar, they look from a different generation. Unfortunately, the creekside dipping pools made from natural rock and hot springs were closed due to the major runoff season this year. I imagine those pools is how the facility started. You can cross the creek on a neat bridge to quieter, adult-friendly pools on the other side. They've recently added an upper play pool including a waterslide and other fun amenities. It is a charming place overall and I hope to return.

We rolled in with ease, recharged from our descent and immediately began to pick up information. The woman at the front desk indicated a hotel room was well over $250/night, so we elected for the $20 day pass to use the pools and shower facilities. It might have been the best $20 I spent on the entire trip. We pedaled up to the "fun pool" first because they told us the waterslide was closing soon. Can't let that happen! The attendant let us pull our bikes into the fenced area of the pool deck and we made a good mess of a corner with all of our gear spread to air out. The attendant, nice guy, also added the optional waterslide ticket to our pass, free of charge being so close to closing. Trail magic! We jumped in the shower and I enjoyed a long, hot soak. It's the first time I'd seen myself in a mirror in a good while and things were changing. My mustache and beard looked...rough. My body.... gaunt. My eyes maybe a little sunken, even. *Creepy*, I thought to myself but quickly shook it off. I joined Brad in the pool and found Nirvana. What a relief physically and mentally this oasis was. We took it in for only a few minutes before deciding a few laps down the waterslide was in order. This was so entertaining, silly, and plain fun that neither of us could stop laughing and smiling on the way down. We probably sounded like idiots. Something about putting all of that effort in to this point made the contrast so great. It was a pure delight to be here.

We had some pool drinks (our first of the ride) and slowed time down again, taking in the valley mountain scenery. After a while, we made our way to the lower more historic pools. Now out of the sun, we really laid back and took these in. It was the last moments of comfort we were going to get for a long while.

We had left our bikes just outside the entrance to the old buildings and thankfully found them just the same when we returned. We slowly and sadly put all our gear back on and packed away, knowing we'd need to find camp down the road some distance. A short stop at their gas-station-style convenience store for "dinner" and we saddled up for good.

The hot springs behind us, we pedaled away and back into the spartan but charming accommodations we'd grown to love on the trail. I was honestly enjoying the nights out in camp. We pedaled on a road through the Chalk Creek area for two more miles before finding the proper singletrack again. These roads weren't paved but instead stark white with clear evidence of white runoff from the chalky walls of the cliffs above us. It was an interesting experience to be riding along a white road! All of this rock held the day's heat annoyingly well, but soon enough, we found camp just after the trailhead and the temperatures subsided. We chatted with a few other thru-hikers camped next to us. The creek below provided ample cold water, and we settled into bed after some chain maintenance and a chat with some more of our neighbors.

290 miles complete, 54% of the distance, is underlined three times in my notebook.

"Hey buddy! This Sucks!"
(Segment 14)

Segment 14…. Let me brace myself and get a drink before I dive in.

It's funny how fast things change on the trail. One day, one hour, things are going so swimmingly. Next hour, awful. Segment 14 holds very little love in my heart. Other riders we met agreed, "Yeah, 14 is on our shit list too". There are some sections on the Colorado Trail that appeared to have made no consideration for bikers besides slapping a sticker on the trail marker, "Bikes Approved". This is what makes the Colorado Trail so difficult. The altitude, the length, and the remoteness of the trail all come second to the soul-crushing pushing of your 50 lbs of equipment through seemingly coordinated, relentless obstacles. They are precisely timed to catch bike tires and jam up momentum. We might as well have been dragging our rigs through some of these pushes. It's hard to pinpoint where I hold my grudge for these sections. The volunteers? Not really, they are just maintaining the trail. The original designer? I guess, but they made the trail before bikes were even considered! The lack of evolution? More so, but the CT Foundation will likely just shrug and ask, "So, you want us to make the trail...easier?". That's not what I want, either. It's a tough pill to swallow, we just kept our heads down and the screaming to a minimum. It's clear some parts of the trail considered bikes last...and that's probably just fine with the powers at be. It's not one of the hardest bikepacking trips for nothing…

Sunrise on the chalk walls at the end of the detour and start of Segment 14

Alright, here we go. The morning of Segment 14 was actually quite lovely. We slept well from the warmth of the surrounding chalk rock and river sounds of the nearby stream. I had another blissful bathroom break as the early morning light painted across the enormous white chalk walls we'd passed the night before. Creek baths and outdoor poops, they are so damn invigorating! We had our usual makeshift breakfast and coffee and broke camp. We pedaled off uphill and along a winding trail through a flat, sporadically forested, miniature mesa. We had a tremendous view of the huge chalk walled cliffs to our left, still gloriously lit in the sunrise light. The climb was hard and punchy but not impossible here. The morning was going well.

Cruising through miles 2-5, the area was very similar to our home rides in the Buffalo Creek system near Denver. Fast and easy rolling on hard packed dry dirt, with arid surroundings and almost no underbrush. You could see the bends coming through the trees and rip along accordingly. I was beginning to enjoy the trail and its winding curves at good speed.

PSHHHHHHH! I was rolling along a level section of hard packed dirt trail, sparsely scattered with small angular rocks. I have no idea what I hit, but felt something momentarily grab my rear tire and yank a good tear into the tread. A felt a line of Stan's sealing fluid spray the back of my neck as I heard the puncture shwish-shwish-shwish, rotating behind me as I stopped. I quickly turned the tire to put the tear into the dirt, hoping the extra grit and debris would help the clotting ability of the latex fluid spraying out of the wheel. I worked fast and pushed hard on the leak, but the tear was big, a little bigger than half an inch, and the Stan's fluid was rapidly evacuating the hole despite my best efforts. My pace was feverish and I was searching for answers. It was of no use. My tire bled to death in my hands. I sat down on the side of the trail with my crippled bike and accepted that I just flatted-out. The trail was relatively smooth and I wasn't riding hard at all. I was shocked and searched the trail for a culprit. Nothing. Angry, I began to unpack my repair kit.

I opted to try to bring the tire back to tubeless status. Being in tubeless configuration provides better resistance to (small, clearly) puncture flats and is more tolerant of lower air pressure. I could have put a tube in the tire, but I only had two tubes for the whole trail and considered them my last resort. So, I used a tire plugging kit made by Dynaplug, but it's the first time I'd ever used it. In fact, this was my first puncture flat since moving to Colorado years ago! This device works like the old, tarred "bacon strips" we used to carry around in cars to plug a flat while it's still on the rim. I used the tool to insert two plugs securely into the tear. There was still some Stan's fluid left in the tire, but no air pressure. I unscrewed the valve-core from the rim and squirted in a two-ounce bottle of emergency fluid. I screwed the core back in, said a prayer to the trail gods, and elected to pump instead of using our singular CO_2 cartridge. The tire bead seated on the rim again (a miracle in itself), and the tire grew firm, apparently holding the pressure I applied. A watched nervously as some Stan's leaked from the plugs but then held. Absolute jubilation. The plugs worked just as described. This was great, but I hadn't rolled them on the trail yet. My initial happiness turned to a time-bomb mentality as I thought, "Watch. I'll make it 200 yards down the trail and we'll be back at the drawing board, only with less supplies". Ye of little faith. The plugs continued to hold. We were back in the game.

Little did we know, 'back in the game' soon took on a sadistic twist. Earlier, Brad had a conversation with some thru-hikers coming the opposite direction, northbound, on the CT. They mentioned something along the lines of these segments being "rough country". We found their claims to be true. Not long after the flat, the trail slid into the category of total slog. The singletrack was indeed so rough that we were pushing well more than half the time. The downhills didn't provide much reprieve as the "flow" was absent. Flow is a term used to describe trail construction. Good flow means the trail's descent angle and design is such that the rider's assumed speed isn't obstructed by a tight obstacle, switchback, or other momentum hampering device. Good flow means the pace of the rider is slowly transitioned from high to low speed using varying grades in order to set a rider up for a particular challenge ahead, etc. Bad flow means the designers have installed a huge speed bump, for example, in an otherwise high-speed section. Its less safe and requires exponentially more effort. Perfect flow, theoretically, might describe a rider never having to touch brakes, despite varying speeds, for the entire downhill run! This section was below 2 out of 10 on flow. We'd push and push up and over baseball to grapefruit sized rocks, hill after hill, only to find a downhill on the backside that couldn't be easily ridden and therefore taken advantage of. My God, did we push. Brad and I both suffered dearly.

To top off this excruciating experience, our pace was costing us time. We were delayed into the afternoon and were still climbing in altitude, not descending like we'd planned. As expected, the afternoon thunderstorm boomers began to build all around us. They grew larger, darker, and began to merge. It was only a matter of time. We doubled down on our effort, spending perhaps beyond what we could afford. We left it all in that section, cursing up a storm and taking punches, but not falling down yet. The storm continued to close on us and was directly overhead, flashing and cracking in tight intervals. We put each uncountable ridge behind us one by one and eventually found ourselves fairly exposed on top of the last ridge sixteen miles into this segment. The clouds filled in, and we didn't stop to take a breath. Rain started to spit out from above and the wind was picking up into erratic gusts. Straight over the ridge we went and started the descent. In my camera footage, you can flashes and hear the thunder crack nearby the trail---and my scream of almost nervous laughter. We finally found a section of fair and improving trail on this final downhill portion. It started first as a mellow downhill grade through forest and, though it required pedaling, our speed was excellent. We pushed hard, pedaling downhill on a section we'd otherwise coast. Close and black, the clouds crowded the open valley we plunged into.

Powerlines overhead! I remember looking up at them as they went over, we're getting close to people again! A highway! "It's Highway 50!", I yelled back to Brad. Seeing it, Brad and I flew down the mountainside of chunky service road and singletrack switchbacks toward the blessed pavement. I felt like a monster truck smashing down the trail, suspension and body in harmony, invincible. Highway 50 marks a huge milestone for riders. The beloved Monarch Crest Trail, a highlighted International Mountain Bike Association Epic Ride, begins just up the road from here. Just a mile off the trail, we had sent a resupply box to the nearby Monarch Spur RV Campground. This was familiar ground again. We realized we might beat the storm, the slog was over, and shelter and a meal lay just below. We slashed down the hill with mother nature hot on our heels. After hours of outrageous hike-a-bike, we rolled into the campground with about five minutes to spare before the skies opened up. We ducked into the campground's outdoor, but roofed, social area and regrouped in the rustic surroundings.

Running out to grab a picture before the rain began. Our shelter was the old building left of the newer camp store

We dashed in and out of the shelter to the camp office to retrieve our supply box, ask questions, look at the weather radar, and purchase a Coke and Snickers (naturally). We couldn't fit everything we sent ourselves onto our bikes so we prioritized. We ate what we could right there and sent some items back home in the box. I inspected my bike and replaced my rear set of brake pads that had become dangerously low. I had brought a set with me in my repair kit as well as sent a set in the box. I will end up using both sets before we finished the CT. Our bikes were absolutely fully brimmed now. We thought the bikes were full when we rolled in, but creativity reigned and we packed more food under every strap we had. Ahead was 4 days of hard alpine riding and meals accordingly before we'd get into Silverton.

Brad was eager to leave, I was reluctant. We both regained our superhuman Snickers strength at the campground and were ready for the second half of the day, but it wasn't energy on my mind. The dark sky remained above the mountains and the next section was a fair distance spent above tree line. It had stopped raining but I knew the risk still remained. I thought our chances of getting whacked on the hill were elevated, even more so than the last section while we were chased. I was not a happy camper. The thought of getting fused to my carbon frame was upsetting! I spent a lot of money on this bike, dammit! I couldn't get a read on the weather's progress and I prefer my weather neat and tidy. I think Brad took the ignorance-is-bliss, what's-with-all-the-negative-waves method and just wanted to send it.

Fine.

I stalled as long as I figured reasonable and we packed up and left. The campground owner gave us a cautious farewell (thanks, pal, so stoked with your confidence) and I closed my eyes and put my balls back into my riding shorts. We pedaled out of the campground uphill on Highway 50. I looked above me, and then didn't look any more. I put my head down and got to work.

Monarch Crest, King for a Reason
(CT West + Segment 15)

Those closely familiar with the CT will have noticed by the title that, yep, we detoured off the trail. Damn right we did. We're *biking* and we weren't about to let one of Colorado's best rides go unridden when we were right next to it.

Monarch Crest Trail is a section alpine singletrack that becomes a destination during seasonal months. It typically begins with a hired van ride up to Monarch Pass and is directional, ending far lower in Poncha Springs. From the pass, the trail ventures well above the tree line for many miles before rocketing back down with some great gnarly sections and grip-and-rip descending. The trail is 36 miles long and takes a full day to drive out, ride, and return home. With a short open season and limited shuttle permits available, mountain bikers from all around venture to this very spot to knock it off their lifetime bucket list. We'd both ridden it before and knew it was too good to pass up.

We got back onto Highway 50 and began grinding uphill, quickly passing the exit of segment 14 on our right and the beginning of segment 15 on our left. Remember, we have been riding on the Collegiate East segment of the trail until now. We continued uphill past the CT blazes and pointed toward Monarch Pass and the *CT West* section. The East-West division was nearly complete now, CT West lay just ahead at the pass. We thought we'd have the wheels to power up to the pass. Our energy was spent, unplanned, running from the storm of segment 14 and so we came to a resolution.

We stuck out thumbs out.

In short order, trail magic struck harder than lightning, and a gorgeous, white, full size F-250 King Ranch truck with leather seats, air conditioning, and a bike rack veered off the highway in front of us, delivered by angels. A stocky dad, highly animated and with a wild Einstein head of brown hair and his two teenage sons, dirty from long days of riding themselves, piled out of the truck.

"Jesus Christ! You guys want some help?! We thought you were gonna be heroes and crank out this climb until your thumbs popped out and we all looked at each other and said, 'These fellas are in trouble!'". I dubbed this hysterical trio, Team Coal Stoke. The father and sons team had their own bikes packed in the bed of the truck. They'd been out all freaking summer riding all over the United States, non-stop, spending a week here or there before moving to the next state. They rattled off all the big-hitter parks and major trail systems they'd been to and we were amazed. They did it so right, an incredible adventure of grade-A bonding time. We described the details of our undertaking as best we could, and were looking into three sets of wide-open eyes of awe while we did it. I think we were mutually impressed with each other's endeavors. I definitely have a family mountain bike park tour on the bucket list now. They were a riot. An intense rush of classic bro-talk complete with high fives and fist bumping. When hardcore mountain bikers help other hardcore mountain bikers, it's like your best friends are in trouble and you'll give them the pep talk of their lives to get them back on their feet. That was us, getting the pep talk and sharing the stoke of their total success. They boosted us the 8 miles to the top of Monarch Pass and boosted our morale even farther.

Team Coal Stoke unloading my bike at Monarch Pass. Thanks a million guys!

We rolled in on four tires to the top of the Monarch Pass, disembarked, and shook hands with Team Coal Stoak. They wished us well and we headed up to the scenic chairlift station that those three passed only hours ago. I remembered I dared to look up at the sky and to my relief the clouds were thinning. The CT delivers another wild swing to the experience.

We passed behind the iconic lift station and started up and along the Collegiate West and Monarch Crest Trail with a good grind up a double track road into the trees. The trail breaks off the road to the right and runs through sub-alpine pines at a level grade and good speed. It makes for a nice break after the grinder climb. Eventually, the singletrack resumes a chunky, low-speed, rock garden climb and in short time we left the trees below us and savored the open alpine views we loved in this section.

Brad at the beginning of the singletrack of Collegiate West and the co-located Monarch Crest Trail

The reason we decided to follow this route of the trail was a double-feature. We enjoyed the intense alpine scenery and legendary trails of Colorado straight off of Highway 50. In addition, our route prevented us from burning out completely in the harsh Foose's Creek hike-a-bike. We've heard the Foose's Creek is a monster effort. It's another, possibly worse push than we'd already experienced that day. We heard this small modification from Bikepacking.com and we appreciated it.

After crushing out the last of the climb over soft-ball sized and shaped loose rocks (not all of the Monarch Trail is blissful), we crested the high point and took in the view as our old friend, the Collegiate East section, met us again at the East-West's southern junction. Again, another simple sign, this time with a more majestic setting. This sign marked the southern merge of these two options to make the Colorado Trail whole again. We snapped a few milestone pictures. It really feels like we're accomplishing the trail, despite the huge effort. Amazingly to me, the markers hat before were only in my head are passing by in reality. I feel almost heroic. Regardless of how off the original plan we've become, it's still working.

The Collegiate West-East southern junction marker

We rode the Monarch Crest Trail until the CT diverted off the prescribed 36-mile route we'd known and ridden before. As the trail works its way into the forest, we picked up speed with the design improvements. Eventually, it dumps onto a rowdy service road. Rowdy because of the whoops from rain drainage! We jumped these as high as we dared again! Our brakes were well warmed and our minds relieved to have such an intense day behind us. Seeing Marshall Pass's roads and signs below, we'd made it through another day.

Brad climbing behind me to the top of the trail (above). I salute my partner for a job well done, downhill from here (below).

As we pulled into the Marshall Pass parking area, a large crowd (relatively, probably about 25) of teenagers were mingling around with tents and a roaring campfire. This was the first encounter we had with any kind of "crowded" camping and didn't really know what to make of it! They laughed and chatted along with each other at the fire. Some made runs to and from their tents. We figured they were a young group of friends likely all "sleeping at each other's friend's house" and came out here to smoke weed and get romantic. Luckily, the valley was large and wide and the camping space was big enough to support a small music festival. Our greatest concern was one of them might take a poke at some of our gear. Another first, we found ourselves dodging cow pies on the ground, seemingly everywhere. We looked for the best place we could for the tent and set up shop.

As we went to a nearby stream to wash up and brush teeth, one of the campers asked, "Hey nice Spot, do you like it?". He was referring to my bike's brand and I stopped in for a conversation with him. After we finished our usual explanation of our trip and progress, he explained that all of these campers were part of a high school pre-semester program. Each year, this high school sends its students into the wild on a backpacking trip together! In 4 year's time, they will have finished the Colorado Trail, taking a chunk out before each school year begins. Not only does it get kids to realize there is more to the world than what comes out of their phone, they get to learn about themselves and what they're capable of too. What a program! Brad and I were astounded that this even happens in 2019; the decade of shaming, heli-parents, and lawsuits. This dashed any concerns we had with these fine folks and we chatted up a few of the campers personally. Don't judge a book by its cover: reality series. Brad and I said goodnight and continued past them to take a bath in the creek. This turned out to be a challenging proposition. The creek was soggy with mud and tight vegetation, the water frigid, and students milling about in regular intervals. Not wanting to get a mugshot taken, we took turns playing sentry while the other bathed as fast as humanly possible. Nevertheless, we emerged refreshed and headed back to camp.

This day is journaled in my notebook in messy block letters in full-size Sharpie pen. For whatever reason, the normal fine-tip wasn't putting ink to paper so I scribbled some lines as best as one can with what felt like a telephone pole. There are two lines that stand quite clear:

HITCH TO MONARCH PASS
CHILI-MAC!!!!

Brad brought a bag of chili mac instant dinner and after that day of insane statistics, it was the best goddamn spoonful of food I could have ever hoped for. I think we may have even fortified it with instant mashed potatoes. We gobbled up every morsel. I wish I had 3 more packs to myself. I never noted when they started exactly, but hunger pangs will eventually be something I live with on the trail. The sharp cramps in my upper stomach went so far as to wake me up every few minutes when I slept. It was around this night that they began to come occasionally, picking up with frequency and intensity as the trip continued. This heavenly meal may have been the last time I enjoyed a night's sleep without the pains.

Another cyclist rode into camp and set up his extremely minimal camp in a flash. His "tent" was an open tarp hung in an A-frame fashion, and he crawled into his sleeping bag underneath. Saying little and keeping to himself, we watched him arrive and fall asleep in a matter of minutes. Brad and I looked at each other and wondered who the idiots were here, us or him. Just a different approach to bikepacking I guess.

Jordan and I actually connected for about 30 minutes via texting that night. Every other night or so, Brad and I would try to see if there was any signal where we camped. There wasn't enough signal for a phone call here, but texting requires far less data and often gets by on a shoddy connection. We were successful and I slept better having gotten to hear her voice again, even if it was only her words plus my imagination. What a day, again. Remember, earlier today I had the flat. We'd come a long way once more.

"Brad, we're going to get vaporized."
(Segment 16)

I sat up in my sleeping bag this morning to the sound of cows in the distance. The campers next door were still sound asleep. I slept fairly well that night and it was another beautiful day to start, the mornings often were. I looked into my data book and realized Sargents Mesa was up next on the hit list. I had read other's reviews of this upcoming area and, while the views were great, the trail reports were not kind. It might become another day of trouble.

Brad unzipped the tent door and we were greeted with a cow's ass. We looked around and the cows were everywhere, moving in slowly and unstoppably. We laughed and watched curiously and cautiously to make sure none snuck up behind Brad or I and nipped us in the bud. Could you imagine? "What happened? Why didn't you finish?". "...I got my ass beat by a cow".

These aren't the same cows from camp as described, but an example of one of many times we passed a herd

We finished our usual morning routine as our biking neighbor did the same. For all the time we took to get ready, he laid in his bag drinking tea and looked at the sunrise. However, to our surprise he was nearly ready to start pedaling as we rolled out of camp. He was silent and unreadable. We still couldn't decide if he was a genius for making his system work on so little, or a masochist.

I have to admit my brain has fully deleted large parts of the pushing memories of this trail. The foggy areas are growing wider as I write this and I rely more on my trail notes as each segment passes by. Heading up to Sargents Mesa was another day that I knew we pushed intensely, but I honestly can't remember it. I remember the highlighted searings of these sections, which I'll describe next, but I can't bring myself to fabricate memories I don't have. All I can tell you is that I have a loathing sense in my head for this area as I look back and try to remember what it looked like and the situation we were in. MTBProject.com gives this segment an *Extremely Difficult* double black diamond rating. My notebook reads, *36 miles, 6180 ft. Really hard day physically and mentally. Tough, extreme pushing in [Sargents] Mesa* and my Strava log reads, *Sargents Mesa. By far the new hardest segment.*

Climbing up to Sargents Mesa we got a nice warning to go with the tremendous views

Sargents Mesa and the remainder of segment 16 and 17 spend the entire length above 10,000 feet and I'd estimate almost two thirds above 11,000. To top that off, the nice sunrise we had that morning had quickly become a "Red Sky in the Morning…" situation. The clouds again rolled in and thickened.

Before we reached the mesa, we passed through a deeply rutted set of trails in an OHV area. That stands for Off-Highway Vehicle and designates an area in which dirt bikes and other recreational motorized vehicles are approved for use on the trails. The fun in a motorized vehicle is that you can search for intense challenges of what terrain you can overcome. Some of the trails are quite steep and so you a rider uses the engine to power up and over the obstacles. This usually creates a degree of wheel-spin that ends up digging the trail incrementally deeper between rocks, etc. Eventually you end up with trail that is 'moto-ed' out. It becomes so deep and crevassed that the trail generates its own impassibility. We found ourselves unable to move over these trails without pushing and even climbing up onto boulders. Some of the climbing and descending sections that were eroded worst were worthy of a trials competition. It would have been easier to ride straight through the woods, sans trail, than follow the trail here.

As we slogged along, pushing mile after mile, the thunder began. Overhead I could hear thunder cracking routinely. It's an awful sound when you're that high in elevation. We were climbing up through 11,000 feet and finishing segment 16 to the tune of constant rumbles. We had been in higher elevations throughout this segment, but now the brewing storms were adding a fresh twist to the danger. I made my concerns public. Brad didn't seem very phased by what I had to say. I could understand slightly, there was no bolts coming out of the sky and disintegrating trees around us. All of the lightning so far was cloud-to-cloud, thankfully. The thunder continued to come out of the sky directly above us. I knew that this was fine and well until the bolts decided they'd had enough fun with the clouds and took aim at the mountain we were on. If that occurred, we stuck out like sore thumbs and we didn't exactly have a high speed means of ducking into shelter---that didn't exist. We'd be along for the ride, rolling the dice.

At some point on the trail, the climb was interrupted temporarily by a short switchback descent on rocky and steep trail. The boulders were big and numerous and we were forced to pick our way through while teetering on our bikes. I remember being about twenty yards ahead of Brad and stopped to watch his progress through the heavy rock gardens. Just as I turned around and looked up, I saw Brad nose into a rock and high-side over his bike in a spectacular crash. His bike fell away downhill and wiped his legs out from under him. As he was going down his limbs shot out instinctively to catch himself or anything around him. He fell, butt and back first, right on his flat frame. As he dropped onto the rocks, he went out of sight over the lip of the trail above me. The sound of carbon into stone and Brad's groan stopped my heart. I dropped my bike and started running back of the trail, but Brad quickly called out that he was ok. I stopped and asked if he was sure and he replied, "Yeah…. Goddammit…". He was picking himself up and inspecting his bike. "Dude, I cracked my handlebars". My heart sank and I thought, *Oh no, we're done*. I pictured him holding a foot's worth of his handlebars in his hands, controls and all, separated from the bike. I started walking up the trail again, but was surprised to see him round the switchback above me on his bike and roll my way. He stopped next to me as I looked him over worried and bewildered. He showed me his handlebars and I almost laughed. The very end of his bars, outboard of the grip, had split on a rock and took the shape of a miniature clock tower bell. Only the most outboard inch of his bars had a crack, the rest of the handlebars was just fine. "Oh! This isn't too bad at all!", I said. We were very lucky that Brad's bars were aluminum. Aluminum is more prone to deforming, while the lighter carbon composite, although stronger, tends to fail completely when overstressed. I explained my confusion and he replied that both he and his bike were still good to ride. I guess in the end we should have seen this as an omen.

And yet, we pushed on. It's almost embarrassing for me to look back on. In my life I've done some things that might be out of many people's comfort zones, but I choose the things I participate in wisely so I can manage risk. I had tried to let go of that uptight mentality for this ride in total but this is one section I wish I had not. After Brad's crash, we should have reconsidered. With the thunder rolling above, we pressed. I dashed as fast as I could muster from one patch of trees to the next, hoping the electrons weren't gathering on my helmet. I'd get to the next tree line and turn to find my partner's pace as constant as ever as he progressed through the open Mesa. I was flabbergasted, frustrated, and angry I was in this position. I was convinced either I or he had a betable chance at having to carry a charred riding partner out of the backcountry.

We were still in the climb of Segment 17 when the skies opened up with hail. We could see it coming up the Mesa in a hazy wall of precipitation. Like a cartoon, hail bounced off Brad's head and apparently woke him out of his pushing and grinding daze. He exclaimed, "Shit, we need to get to some shelter or something! It's really going to start coming down!". He turned ninety degrees off the trail and split for the closest trees available, leaving me again jaw agape on the trail. Thunder with a chance of vaporization were apparently no match for the hail problem we now had. It was maddeningly comical to watch that transformation take place.

The hail did come down and it came down hard and for a long time. I ran into the trees after Brad to get some initial protection from the hail. We rushed to get something more helpful set up. Brad pulled out our protective tent footprint and I strung up a cord between two trees which he could throw it over. This A-frame idea looked great until we both tried to get under it. The shelter area was too small and our bikes and half our bodies were exposed to the elements. We did a quick debate if it was worth it to get the entire tent out. It was already getting slushy and soggy with melting ice and water. We didn't want to open our bags and expose all our gear just to get the tent out and put it onto slushy grass. We decided it wasn't worth the effort and we'd ride out the hail until the storm passed. How long does a hail storm last? 10 minutes? Less?

Brad and I in our makeshift insta-shelter while the hail is coming down

We stood, shoulder to shoulder, huddled in our riding gear and slowly getting soaked and chilled to the bone. The hail lasted for almost 45 minutes and then continued with rain. We sulked in our poor luck, if you could call it that. We looked at each other, and looked out into the open mesa. The hail was 3/8th of an inch big and ended up covering the ground to almost an inch of slush and ice. Perfect riding conditions. The thunder and rain continued above as hail subsided and the wind picked up. We wondered what we could do as we started to freeze. The hail and rain cooled the air temperature down fast and we shivered under the tarp. I donned my raincoat and Brad used his to protect his bike's bags and gear that weren't under the tarp. I walked around examining the new trail conditions. Slick and sloppy, full of slush and mud. It would be a hard ride against the elements if we decided to leave now, but staying meant freezing in this forest. We had to get moving, even just to get warm, whether we liked it or not.

We stuffed the tarp away and Brad got his rain jacket on. We pointed uphill, yet again, and started a meager climb buffeted by winds. Little did we know, the top of the segment was only about 500 yards away. The top was just as covered as our shelter spot, but we could make easier rolling progress. We continued and our pace picked up as the trail began to descend and the slush thinned. Had we known this we would have just pushed over the top from the beginning! We hadn't any idea how far we were from the highpoint of elevation and not paying attention here cost us dearly. We were stripped of any morale we had remaining and were cussing up a storm. This wasn't just getting caught in a storm, it was a soaking, freezing, blowing slushy mess that we couldn't keep to the outside layers of clothing. As we descended, I noticed an odd shape in the woods to my right. As I glanced over, deep in the woods, I saw the same open A-frame tarp and bike from the camping neighbor we had the night before. The man was motionless, sitting in his bag inside, and holding a mug. This second mysterious sighting was making this person more into an apparition. I was transfixed for a moment as I wondered who this quiet woods-walker was, and how he got there in the first place. I never saw him pass us. I didn't say anything to Brad, I didn't know if I dreamt it.

As we furthered downhill on the trail, the wet dirt dried to only damp but our attitudes didn't improve. Not long after

I sighted the rider, I realized Brad must have seen him too because he suggested we needed a warm-up break. Even though we were riding again, I myself was unable to produce any heat since the hail storm so I agreed. We found a sloping area of thick ground vegetation with a patch of trees to block the wind. It would have to do, even though the ground greens and grass were still covered in water. We pitched the tent, grabbed our sleeping bags and pads and all the clothing we had, climbed in and zipped up. We were two thickly dressed burritos in less than a minute. I felt some security return as my body began to slowly warm, and that allowed me to nod off. We both fell asleep to clear our heads, try to reset, and gain some much-needed rest.

Falling Flat
(Segment 17)

About an hour later we woke to a warmer tent with a little ray of sunlight hitting the rain covered canopy. The air outside was still cold but the wind had calmed and sunlight poked through now and then. I too was warmer, but not dry nor was any of my gear. Regardless, this stop gave us a little boost and allowed us to rally and continue the push. We slowly packed up our gear, trying to shake off as much water as we could, and headed back up to the trail.

The apparition was waiting for us. Alone, with his thin bike and a bag or two, the man started to talk to me before I even got to the trail. I don't remember exactly what he said because of the strangeness of this interaction. It was something along the lines of "Hello there! I was sitting in my tent admiring my bike, they are such wonderful inventions of technology, when I noticed I have a broken spoke! Look here, I've duct taped it together hoping this will keep it from poking a hole in my rim tape and causing me to flat". This was our first interaction. I said I was sorry to hear that and tried to sympathize for a minute with him. He asked if we were going the whole way and I said yes. He explained, "I just kinda dick around in the mountains here until I've had my fill and I'll head out. With this spoke thing I don't know what I'll do now. Maybe I'll bail out to [some small town], there is a good guy there, [Bob], who owns a bike shop and repaired [some other problem] I had a few years back". Such an interesting creature. We chatted for a few more minutes as I tried to take this fellow in. Jolly Roger was actually overall a bit of a negative Nance. He created a strange oxymoron of complaining in an upbeat fashion. Nevertheless, he seemed unphased by his impending breakdown but simply had to tell someone. I don't remember if he rode a 27.5" or 29" sized wheel but I do remember looking at his hubs and realized neither Brad's nor my spoke design matched his hub format. I would have gladly given him one if it did, I packed three spares. Either way, he was already hoping to keep his wheel from going flat at all and didn't seem interested in repairing the rim on the trail. He would have to bail out in my opinion. The flat danger he described was very real and his rim would probably only get more and more out of shape as the stresses moved into the surrounding spokes. Eventually it would crumble. We were in one of the most remote sections of the CT and I hoped he would make it to civilization ok. We said good luck and farewell and continued down the trail in front of him. It would have been worth looking back over my shoulder to make sure he was indeed real.

3 miles later I heard the dreaded sound of air leaking. I stopped immediately and scanned my bike to find a wad of trail debris stuck to my tire where the sealing fluid was spraying. It was the same damn spot as before. The plugs I had installed into my rear tire, only yesterday, were leaking fluid and air at an alarming rate. I immediately looked back up the trail, half expecting the man with the broken spoke to be holding his bike over his head, casting voodoo on us below! So coincidental it was spooky. I focused my anger of the day on my tire. I muttered and cursed under my breath as I removed my repair kit and dumped its contents onto the damp ground. I kept the repair kit in the very bottom of my zip-tie-stitched bag. This means I have to pull out my water reservoir and chain care bag and twist my arm to get to the very bottom where the repairs are stored. It also allows ample time to vent while you're spreading your belongings on the trail just to get to

the bag you want. I pulled out my plug kit and inserted the last 4 of my plugs into the hole and trimmed them. One of the original plugs had fallen out and was causing the leak. Now, 5 plugs were smashed extra tight in the slice and I hoped this would...seal the deal. I exhausted my final bottle of emergency Stan's fluid into the rim for insurance and screwed the valve core back into the stem. If we had any more flats after this, we'd resort to tubes. I pumped air into the tube, saving our CO_2 cartridge again, and prayed. It held, and better than before.

I sat on the trail for a minute after I was done to clear my head. Brad boosted my spirits and coaxed me to realize that this is just one of those things we'll have to deal with. I appreciated his picking me up and I needed it. I'm clearly the more emotional of the two of us. Something I pride myself on is being able to fix many mechanical things. Having this leak come back to bite me was a small and rather petty problem, but I was fumingly annoyed. I got back up on my feet and we carried on.

Light was fading as we worked our way through the remaining teeth in the elevation profile. We pushed some more, rode some more, wash, rinse, repeat until we were connected with a jeep road and began the descent to the end of the segment. We picked up pace and we approached Lujan Pass. Beyond the pass, we descended on the road with Lujan Creek descending alongside. The temperatures plummeted as we got deeper into the valley below and soon we were frigid again. In hindsight, I should have put all my gear on before we started the descent, however, we were so exhausted that it was a hard sell to not just race down the road and into camp. So, for the second time that day I again approached hypothermia as we descended on the road. I've never been colder on my bike than that moment.

We flew past some thru-hikers that were also exhausted and looking for a camp. We wanted some finality to the day badly but also needed some water as well. Further into the bottom we descended and further the temperatures dropped. In the last light of the evening, we reached a gate at the bottom of the jeep road and crossed the intersecting Highway 114 marking the end of Segment 17. Still without water we descended into the very bottom of this open meadow, in the first quarter mile of Segment 18, and found a flat, wet grassy area with Lujan Creek meandering through it.

I knew we'd reached camp and dropped my bike in relief. I was shaking head to foot while I clumsily dug out my headlamp. With our two beams of light we revealed the entire area around us was saturated in cow pies. There was almost as many cow pies as there were clumps of grass. We searched for a poop-free place to pitch the tent and chucked our sleeping gear inside. We found a place that was as suitable as it could be, kicked away the major clods, and we put down the tent's footprint as a poop barrier to our tent itself. We chewed on some cold "dinner" and tried to pack as many calories as we could before bed. I had a hard time finding the energy and motivation to keep eating. We ignored the rest of our nightly chores in favor of simply getting warm and getting to bed. It was a miserable evening of frigid, shaking, foggy breathed, numbed limb existence. We zipped up the door of our tent for the night, and that was a huge mistake.

Freezing Temps and Rain Inside
(Segment 18)

Brad's frosted gear, our soaked tent, and me with my sleeping bag shawl

A water drop fell onto my closed left eye and brought me out of my light sleep. I had been waking up every few minutes from hunger pangs and the cold creeping into my bag, but the drop was a red flag. I blinked the water out of my eyes and focused on the tent around me. I found the entire inside of the tent was covered with large, uniform water droplets. I looked around the tent and saw my sleeping bags footbox and left arm wet. There was water in some of the gear I stored near my head to include my phone, Rylo camera, and notebook. I put my head back on my makeshift pillow and closed my eyes again, "F---". I knew what this would mean for our near future. I woke Brad up slowly and warned him to stay away from the walls of the tent. He cussed as well as he found his bearings. We gingerly started to pack our gear up while staying clear of the saturated tent walls and canopy. Once we unzipped the door, something that should have stayed partially open all night, we realized the extent of our problem.

We camped ourselves in a frigid, frosted, open valley brimmed full with cow poop. There was poop in every direction as far as the eye could see, lining Lujan Creek, and under all of our gear. Every inch of the valley floor was covered in a thick layer of frost from the night before. Our bikes, bags, and gear outside of the tent were also crispy. What a mess. What a mistake. I looked at my compass, 34 degrees Fahrenheit.

We moved everything out of our tent and into a position to dry. The air outside was far colder than inside the tent. The benefit of keeping the tent door shut was that we probably got a better night's sleep keeping the tent's internal temperature above our sleeping bags' ratings. The disadvantage is obvious. Everything seemed wet. I wore my bag like a shawl trying to stay warm and keep it off the wet and frozen grass. The valley walls prevented us from gaining any benefit from the sun until late in the morning. We didn't feel like we had a choice except work to dry out our gear and wait for the sun to finish the job. Brad and I began to wipe out the tent and the rest of our gear. Eventually, our bandanas and mini towels were saturated too and our hands frozen. We couldn't do much more.

Our freezing, poop-filled, valley campsite finally getting some sun. It appears fairly pleasant until you inspect closer and find the cow pies.

We set up our gear to catch the sun's rays when they came and we walked off to find some cleaner water. We had camped directly adjacent to Lujan Creek, but we both believed the water was badly contaminated from the surrounding poop problem. We began to walk along the creek upstream. Highway 114, the road we were on for just a moment last night, crosses Lujan Creek further upstream in the meadow using a large earthen buildup. The creek passes through this pile with a few corrugated pipes. We figured the closer we got to that, the cleaner the water, and we filled our bags and bottles from here.

We returned to camp and shared a breakfast of hot biscuits and gravy out of a pouch. The warmth of this meal helped bring warmth back to our fingertips and toes. The sun finally crested over the hills but was hidden by a layer of clouds. We couldn't catch much of a break this morning and were again demoralized by the persistent cold and lack of drying. We waited for our gear to dry but ran out of patience. Eventually we packed up, much of our stuff still fairly wet and hours of daylight burned, and headed off on Segment 18.

Segment 18 itself was actually a great ride. It was much needed relief from the recent slogs we'd driven through. The long sweeping curves of doubletrack and singletrack was an easy accomplishment. Besides a short but very hard pushing climb, we breezed through this section with relative ease and this set us up well for the La Garita detour that appeared next to impossible on paper. In fact, after about 5 miles into the 13-mile segment, the grade changes to a relatively consistent, very slight downhill slope. This pace of riding is really a treat. The frustration with the Colorado trail is you spend hours and hours pushing up a climb for say 10 miles, and then fly through an equivalent 10 mile downhill in 30 minutes. The satisfaction required to put in the hard effort is not fulfilled by the *short time* riding downhill. Having a constant gentle slope that provides ample time of enjoyable effort on nice trail has become the golden hope for perfect trail out here.

While we rode along Segment 18, we ran into familiar faces of some hikers that passed us while we were unable to ride through the hail-ridden trails of yesterday. It sounded like most people suffered a rough and cold night just like us. At least the trail wasn't singling us out!

60 Miles, 6000 Feet, and a Another Miracle
(La Garita Wilderness Detour)

We'd fully warmed up and returned to our normal level of suffering by the end of Segment 18 and it was time to tackle the behemoth that was the La Garita Detour. Nearly 60 miles in distance, and almost 6000 feet of elevation gain, this made up the second half of our day on the trail. The detour's elevation profile includes two distinct and huge climbs that needed conquering. The profile first slowly dips to 9000 feet before climbing the first tooth to 10,500. It then immediately descends again further to 8,900 feet and again climbs to over 11,500 feet. Another short descent and short climb would finish off the detour at Spring Creek Pass. We knew that ending at a pass means you're climbing out to the finish. What an afternoon this was going to be.

The detour started on wide graded dirt road in an incredibly wide and shallow, featureless valley of light gray and cream color. The hills seemed so far away that it felt almost moonlike in contrast with the intensely sharp and rugged topography of the trail we'd known. These changes were always fascinating to me. Colorado truly holds an immense number of environments to explore. We pedaled along the initially flat road in fairly high gear and made good time. An outdoorsman passed by us with his truck and we asked for some guidance on the area. Really, I think we were asking if he'd give us a ride to our next spot! At this point of exhaustion, we weren't above asking for help on the detours and found the idea of swiping off 6000 feet of road climbing more appealing than the excuse of getting assistance. He couldn't really describe the area well and his truck was stock full of gear and so we couldn't see a way for him to help if he wanted to. Which he didn't! The road passed a few stagnant ponds with some vault toilets nearby. We wanted to fill our water but not from the marshy rims of these ponds. We happened to spot an old hand pump near one of the ponds and filled up there. We'd been filtering our water every time we topped off and this was no different.

As we were pumping, guess who showed up! The thin man with the thin bike. He rolled in and exclaimed, "Good! I see you found the pump! Getting water just fine I hope?". We laughed at replied no problems but said there was quite a bit of contamination in the water and we decided to filter. He responded, "Oh yeah, there is always floaters in that pump, but I just drink it straight anyway. Haven't had a problem". I was curious as to how many times he's passed this specific pump and used the water to have a large enough sample size to claim that with confidence. We chatted some more and I can't make any more sense of his travels besides he is truly just a wandering soul on a bike. He loves this area and frequents it often. His bike was nice and modern as was all of his equipment. In fact, it was largely higher tech and clearly lighter and more compact than ours. It seemed like he could make good time and enjoy the trail on almost nothing. He was the 2019 cycling John Muir---going into the woods with a loaf of bread and some jerky, and emerging two months later just fine with tales to tell. Another fun character of many that the CT provided along its spectrum.

We said farewell wondering, again, if we'd see him in the future. Time would tell I suppose. We continued down the road passing ranches and residences far in the distance on either side. Soon we rode past the Old Agency Work Center, a landmark of the historic Indian reservations in the area, and the Old Agency Ranch, a modern retreat for Colorado ranching style accommodations and experiences. These facilities marked the beginning of the long first climb of the detour. We put our heads down and got to work.

The dirt road luckily remained very rideable and well graded. This was in direct contrast to the very rugged terrain around and we were happy to be on the road. This only dulled the edge of first 1,500-foot climb. The climb continuously steepened until the end of the haul. We didn't have to push on this climb, but it did end in a first gear grade. Eventually we proved victorious and got our bikes over the top of the ridge. We descended fast down to the bottom of the gulley and were surprised to find a few residences nestled deep into this isolated area. We gazed around at their properties as we passed and marveled at how easily it would be to get totally snowed in back here. Wintertime might prove to be an Alaskan style living despite this area being only a few hours driving to major civilization. Our energy levels were again sapped. We took a break to fill our water and eat a snack as we crossed Cebola Creek. We'd been rationing food since the Monarch Spur Campground in an effort to ensure that we'd have enough food to make it to Silverton. We'd been burning a huge number of calories but not consuming our fair share. This was especially true as of recent because of the rough nights and mornings we'd been subjected to. Unable to make up for this deficit, the constant lack of calories ate away at our ability to punch back at the mountains. We rode away from the creek and started back into the mountains.

The view from the crest of the first major climb on the detour

We pedaled along the flat before the next climb with immense and steep jagged rock walls on each side of the road. We knew the road would again steepen as we approached the beginning of the second major climb. This climb alone would consist of more than 2,500 feet. The canyon continued to close in around us as we pedaled further. Our pace began to slow and we had to start downshifting. Just one gear at first, then a handful of gears. Our resolve again weakened on empty stomachs and we actively began talking about how we could find a faster way to the top. Only an hour after we started our conversation (that was a short amount of time on the CT), two trail-running angels literally bolted out of the woods and crossed the path in front of us, headed for their car. Brad turned around to look at me and I was already nodding. I'll readily admit that by this time in our trip, we were hurting bad. We'd put an incredible number of miles behind us, but we were certainly deteriorating. This was our best chance for the help we desperately needed.

Paul and Katie ran into our CT experience with athletic prowess. They were a fit young couple that clearly had energy to spare judging by their jog out of a good length of trail run. The stereotype was fulfilled when we met their dog Asha in the back seat of their Subaru Forester. We introduced ourselves, shared pleasantries, and began the awkward dance in conversation to bring up the fact that we'd desperately appreciate a ride to the top of this road. Their car was clearly full and with no room for two full bikes let alone two grown men. Understandably Katie was trying to be helpful but was hesitant. What could they really do? Paul remained mostly quiet as we hemmed and hawed about what could be done. Brad and I knew we could hold onto the car's open window frame of the door and get towed up the hill. However, proposing this to the couple would be overextending a bit, at least in my opinion. We'd be asking strangers to allow dirtier strangers to hold onto their personal vehicle as they pull us up the dirt road at good speed. Paul still seemed a hard sell to help us at all, but we helped Katie conclude that we could hold onto their car. Once we had agreed that the mission could probably be done, we turned and looked at Paul. "Seems safe enough", he replied. Just like that we had our blessing.

Totally excited, we positioned ourselves on either side of the car, grabbed onto the B-pillar of their Forester, and we precariously accelerated out of the small parking lot. The plan was working! Brad and I had to split our attention between holding a conversation with Katie and Paul and riding uphill on rough road, one-handed, managing the strong and asymmetrical pull of their car! What a riot, it was the most I've concentrated in days. The road was not particularly wider than their Forester, making things even more interesting. I had forgotten to unlock my front suspension's lockout from the road climb. The front fork of my bike was rock hard as I bumped and bounced along the thin shoulder next to their car. Trying to manage the steering, keeping my handlebar well clear of their door, and muster the strength to hold on with the fading grip in my hand was an entirely new challenge I didn't expect. More than once we had to bail off the car as the road thinned and the shoulder disintegrated below into basketball sized boulders. Brad and I looked at each other over the car smiling and laughing with wide eyes. Paul and Katie were camping at one of the sporadic campgrounds up the road toward the pass we were headed for. They were extremely generous to give us a lift at all, and even further extended themselves to pass their campground and to our destination. Our arms burned and our focus faded but with only minor difficulty, and a few restarts, we held on to the top. We crested the last hill and came upon a group of four other thru-bikers who, seeing our tow conclude, immediately commenced a proper ribbing and shaming. They had pedaled to the top and earned the right, so we rode over and let them give it to us. We didn't care one bit.

In all that commotion we never were able to properly thank Katie and Paul for their generosity. Brad and I still feel guilty about this. Their tow was one of about three points in the ride where the interaction of others saved our ride entirely. We were hurting so bad and they came through and became our heroes. I hope someday they read this and know how eternally grateful we are. I'd happily meet them again to buy all of their drinks and show them how far their tow brought us to success on the trail. From Brad and I both, thank you so much.

We met up with these four bikers who were a variable and weathered bunch, just like us. They donned jackets prior to the descent and Brad and I took the hint. I realized this might be another frosty descent like the night before. With my rain jacket in place, we screamed down the newly found pavement like a Tour de France stage. The wind noise made us all descend without a word, it wasn't possible to communicate. Eventually we found the bottom of the long sweeping pavement and started back up again. This was a short climb out of the final few miles of the detour. We chatted as we climbed Highway 149 and compared experiences and bikes and problems and awesome sections and garbage sections. It was fun and invigorating to share some grins and cuss out some sections together. Besides our willingness to accept help on the detours, it sounded like we were having a very typical experience and that helped us rally.

Brad and some of the others rolling into the end of the detour atop Spring Creek Pass

The six of us reached the top of Spring Creek Pass and Brad and I were thrilled to be done. Dusk and layer of clouds was already upon us again and we hustled to find a place to get water and bathe. Spring Creek itself passed on the east side of Highway 149 right off the road. This made a convenient spot to fill our water bags and bottles and get a bath in. We felt great after this bath and crossed the highway and hurried up the hill as the clouds started to sprinkle some rain. We weren't allowed to camp near the parking lot at Spring Creek Pass so we continued west on the trail only slightly. This brought us up a short hill to a flatter area among dead trees. After seeing us figure out the camping situation, the other four riders followed us up the hill and joined us.

Our campsite and sunset after the rain had passed at Spring Creek Pass

We hashed out a quick meal plan for our remaining food until Silverton and promptly cooked up a huge hot dinner. We realized we had enough now to make it comfortably to Silverton and we needed a good pick up. The rain continued to sprinkle and I looked around at the sky with concerns we might repeat a wet tent tonight as well. As I looked up at the troubling sky and near dark conditions, a small Cessna aircraft with its red blinking light puttered by only a few hundred feet overhead through the pass. I thought I was brave to do the trail; this guy was wins for flying in marginal conditions through a mountain pass at night. I took in the distant sunset over the next 20 minutes, with the rain slowly ceasing, and we settled in for some sleep after our bike and camp chores. I looked over my rear tire and the plug was still neat and dry. We were beaten down, but not yet defeated. We're still getting by.

"All Downhill From Here"
(Segments 22)

At 12,592 feet above sea level, Spring Creek Pass welcomed day 11 on the trail with another bitterly cold morning. I wished I looked at the thermometer. Or, maybe not. The temperature swings in the high country were a lurking challenge that always caught up in the mornings. We woke up early and had another ample meal. Of what specifically I can't remember, but it was certainly makeshift. Typically, ingredients allocated for "breakfast" or "dinner" were universal on the CT.

A bitter cold dawn at Spring Creek Pass

Our goal was to get out and crush the day. We were going to need the early start as it was going to be a big one. 7000 feet of climbing over 33 miles. What used to be our biggest singular days of riding back home has now become the usual routine, eleven days in. Those numbers still impress me even months after the trail.

One of the four others took off early to get a head start. It's a good tactic because one can ride ever so slightly slower than the others in his group. The other would slowly make up the time throughout the day. You risk a bit of isolation but your teammates will eventually ride up on you in time. We followed only a short time after him while the last three members were still packing up.

Segment 22 was better. The first section of this trail was a fairly pleasant climb through a wide meadow lined with trees on either side. The grass was green and the trail, although rough, was rideable with a manageable climb. We zig-zagged between these tree bands like pinballs as the trail wandered up the open slope into the blue sky ahead. Similar to many alpine sections, we would occasionally pass a tall post or pole used to mark the trail when the snow inevitably became deep enough to conceal the path.

We kept our heads down and reached a temporary plateau at Jerosa Mesa, completely in the open. There wasn't a single tree on top of this bald field of grass and the views were immersive. 360 degrees around of alpine views with some gorgeously colored mountain ridges in the extreme distance. Their colors of red, orange, and gray reminded me of the fall leaves of my hometown in Ohio. To see these shades spilling out onto a wall of granite scree was a fascinating intersection. The environment was clearly changing as we approached the southern mountains of Colorado. These colors would surround us for the next 100 miles.

The trail quickly deteriorated. This open plateau was filled with football to checked-luggage sized rocks that appeared black and porous. I'm sure there is a logical explanation of how ancient mountain fissures of some tectonic plate heaving in the geopaleoalgabraic era placed these bastards in tight density on this trail. I have two theories: The US Forest Service air dropped these rocks for days in an effort to mitigate hordes of backcountry skiers of future generations, or trail gnomes pushed them out of their underground residences to improve their property value. They were in the millions and freaking everywhere. The rocks prevented us from riding. It wasn't that we *couldn't* ride over and around them as much as the *effort and mechanical risk* we'd subject ourselves to. They continued well into the following downhill to again repeat the demoralizing process the CT had become efficient at. I tried to ride downhill for a short stint but the abuse my bike was taking made me doubt my decision. It was only a matter of time before I smashed carbon into rock and ruined our whole trip. Google "Dragon's Teeth Obstacle", the rocks served the same purpose as these anti-tank fortifications and seemed specifically designed to slow two-wheel progress. Anyone on foot would likely travel through this section almost unimpeded. As with many parts of the CT, this is not so on a 45-inch wheelbase. I pushed all the way to the bottom where the trail intersects a service road that was cleared of this nonsense.

Another panoramic alpine view. Note the boulders in every direction, as described above.

The service road loops around a short hill that hosted a lone antenna array supplied by a few solar panels. I tried to look into who operates in such an intensely remote area and was stumped. My searches only brought up other hikers' suggestion to climb to the antennas to take in the views. That was simply not going to happen in our condition. Bonus miles were out of the question now. We continued past the facility and found after a short descent we came upon the lone ranger that rode out of camp early in the morning. He directed us up a hill to a temporary housing trailer and said it had a few barrels of water that could be used. We needed a fill and so we pedaled our way up to the location. At first, I thought we were being pointed to the Colorado Trail Friends Yurt. This is a round, fabric-walled, rigid tent of sorts that are common in the Rockies. I knew the CT Friends Yurt was in this section and had it marked in my book for consideration to spend the night. This yurt can be reserved, or if there is space, CT travelers can spend a night there to enjoy some relief in a legitimate structure. When we got to the trailer, it was in fact only a workman's housing trailer. I didn't know if anyone was inside but there were recent signs of activity. A log splitting stump, a few tools, and workman's gloves and boots clearly out in the open like they'd been left there to dry. It was a little spooky and we simply didn't know if the 12 or so barrels of water was in fact usable! We eventually broke down and filtered some water into our bags, hoping we weren't stealing it. As we filtered I looked around and spotted a wooden platform structure across a saddle from where we were. I recognized it from pictures of the Colorado Trail Friends Yurt, but there was no yurt on it! Maybe this trailer was a temporary replacement? Maybe it housed volunteers that were working on the missing yurt? I'll never know. Either way, I'm glad we didn't write the yurt into our definite plan for sleeping. What a disappointment that would have been.

I'm glad we bagged some water because the upcoming trail was nothing less than a continuous 7 miles of uphill grinding and pushing up through the tree line once more. We'd push some and grind some and repeat. I only remember the trail nearer to the top of the elevation profile. It was rideable but rocky singletrack that switched back often and was cut into the side of rolling grassy slopes, totally exposed to the sun. Unfortunately, the trail was cut deep vertically and had rising edges of dirt and grass tufts. This became common as the trail moved west and was a real energy sapper. I'm not sure what causes this depth to be honest but it makes riding more difficult. Brad equated it to trying to ride a bike down the gutter of a bowling alley. You bounce back and forth unless you have superhuman perfect balancing skills, which we did not in our diminishing state. The good news was that the views were tremendous. On our grassy hill we were greeted with nearly encompassing mountain views once more. We were very high, almost 13,000 feet in elevation and closing in on a major milestone.

Forced to push in the high altitude well higher than 12,000 feet

We crossed a few precarious snow melts that risked a long slide to the bottom. I was hoping the trail was clear of snow, but I have to be honest, I thoroughly enjoyed the challenge of crossing them. For some reason it added a missing element to our trip I didn't even know I wanted. We hacked steps into the snow and prayed our bikes didn't slip and drag us down the icy slopes. What a blast! It was fun and frankly made me feel like a badass!

Another major hurdle of our climb was a generally short spout of the most extreme terrain of the trip we'd faced yet. The trail, for less than half a mile, turned into an outrageously steep scree scramble. The entire side of the hill was a dump zone of uniform gray broken plates of rock---with a trace of trail barely etched through it. It switched back hard on itself numerous times and created some fairly generous exposure risks. The footing was extremely unstable and the pitch of whole slope was steep enough that a rolling rock would just keep on going to the bottom. The Colorado Trail could have easily circumnavigated this area, but what fun would that be! At times I had my bike fully hauled on my back, I pulled it up by the front wheel, and locked the brakes to use it as an ascending device. Anything I could do to stay on the trail. We moved slowly and we inched out way up and around each steep cut in the mountainside. Brad grew more concerned as we dove into this section. I also admit it was almost overwhelming to work on our own. We picked away at the half-mile, feet and hands on the rock for stability. Eventually, we breathed a sigh of relief when we reached the top. We looked back on that insane stretch and wondered if anyone had the prowess to pedal up, or even down it. I'm almost entirely sure it's never been done.

A typical example of the trail degrading into unclimbable scree. I mean…come on.

Brad and I slowly nibbled away at the rising elevation in front of us. The air was so thin and we had lost the majority of our "punch". Long ago, however, we found our slow burn pace that helped us keep making miles through higher altitudes, even if we weren't winning any land speed records. We chewed along until we saw two other hikers taking a break near a signpost in the trail. I smiled because I knew what it meant. We were far too remote to be passing an intersection. I turned around and Brad was about a switchback behind me and was still getting along just fine. Look at us now! We'd reached the highest point in the entire 550 miles of the Colorado Trail. 13,271 feet above sea level was marked on a basic sign stuck in the ground. The monumental achievement marked by another simple marker made me grin as Brad pulled up. We high-fived and hugged. Our spirits lifted and we took a few more pictures for the memory. We even mustered the strength to raise our bikes over our head in defiance of the extreme trip it had been so far. Looking at the picture it seems so plain, as if it's simply a grassy meadow and we're grinning in front of a pole in the ground. It could have been taken anywhere really. We'd been through much rougher terrain than what surrounded us now and yet we were standing on the highest point well into the alpine zone. It was completely different than I had expected.

Standing proud at the CT's highest point. The sign I hold says "All downhill from here"

"This trail is F&%$#&$ Awful! I WANT A NAME!"
(Segment 23)

After a short break and a few mediocre snacks, we carried on. No time for naps or rest, remember. Section 23 lay ahead in just a few more miles. Being at the highest point, descent was simply inevitable. We rode downhill from the high point for just over 3 miles. It was a nice break and a decent relief before the biggest of the pushes ahead. The trail was skinny at first but opened into a jeep road that remained above tree line. This section was littered with intersecting trails and creeks and the unchecked drainage scars made for more entertaining ramps. The road became wide enough that we could be playful with the bends and curves, picking lines and weaving around each other. The entire area was full of bright color and wildflowers. The steep walls earth was painted yellows, reds, and oranges from the obvious and plentiful mining activity. Deep green areas of grass and low brush and a perfect blue sky completed this image worthy of Ansel Adams. Only a few other outdoorsmen were seen in the distance, zipping around on dirt bikes with their engines muffled in the wind.

How rugged and exposed the trail had become. For scale, Brad is in this picture, on the right, stepped just off the trail.

Note the trail we'd already covered, far behind Brad. Yeah…it was that steep.

The views were tremendous; however, it exposed the pain in store for us. We could easily see the trail, miles ahead, and we groaned as it zigged and zagged up the side of mountain after mountain. It was difficult to keep track of the number of climbs we endured and, even now, the trail becomes foggy. I can remember clearing over passes, pushing up trail cut directly into the side of the mountain, and crossing scree fields that were almost impossible to ride. I cautiously rode through one section of scree and got away with it. The next section I attempted created a total washout including me, my bike, and the trail itself. The rock scree was so delicately spread that once you started sliding downhill, it took some time for you *and the rocks around you* to stop sliding all together. It felt like slipping down a sand dune except with shards of granite! The noise of crossing these strips was strangely acoustic. It made me think of a cartoon playing the xylophone on the rib cage of a skeleton, *tink-bonk-bank-tonk-bink.* Brad spotted two marmots fighting over god knows what in this desolate area and they tumbled clear down the side of the mountain, locked in battle. A long train of falling rocks chased behind them and I looked up our own slope and hoped a marmot didn't start some rockslide-scree-avalanche above us.

I'm walking this section due to the consequence of a long scree slide if an error is made

Up and down, 12,000, 13,000, 12,000, 13,000, *summit ridge...cross creek...reach saddle...follow valley*. We just kept going, one pedal stroke at a time, one 100-foot section at a time. I have in my notes, *Outrageous....Almost impossible*. This was the climax of the two-week epic battle we made for ourselves. Section 23 was the hardest on us. I roared in wide-eyed rage, demanding to know who's at fault, "THIS TRAIL IS F&$%@#% AWFUL! I WANT A NAME!". The sinister mountains weren't amused. They simply waited for us to continue the test. As my echo returned to me, my explosion was snuffed by the lack of any provocation. I put my head down, submitted, and started pedaling again. We were exhausted and starving, probably literally. It was perhaps the most effort I'd ever put out in a single day in my whole life. We started at sunrise and already cleared 20 miles of almost all climbing.

We were fading faster than the trail was passing under us. I knew we were done. Our plan was to resupply and get dinner in Silverton and then head out to find camp just outside town. I pulled out my inReach satellite messenger and typed my wife's number in.

"We need a room in Silverton. I need you to book something cheap for a single night tonight. We're not going to make it out of town. Still making progress, but not well"

Brad was close to physical exhaustion. It was the closest he had been to exhaustion since we started. I wasn't fairing any better, at 5% or less left. My brain was definitely out of order because I couldn't keep track of the miles anymore. I think I told Brad that we were less than a mile from the top more than once. I simply couldn't make sense of what was going on. We seemed at the highpoint and I'd look at the elevation profile of the trail ahead, hoping for good news. The way I was reading it provided hope. I analyzed a section of downhill followed by a flat, then down the road into Silverton. We seemed home free, on our way to a long descent. But after the descent, the trail met the mining road to Stoney Pass. I was flabbergasted to look up a long, hot, chalky road of gravel and rocks to climb to the pass and more than double the distance I estimated. All day I felt like we'd been in our first gear. Brad and I were entering a zombie like existence and close to crashing. Brad had stopped talking or responding to my comments. I was rambling on endlessly about trying to make sense of the data book.

The crest of the road at Stoney Pass. A godforsaken area of inhospitable rock.

My GPS interrupted me and beeped at an incoming message. *"Booked at Prospector's Motel, under your name for tonight. Already paid, $100. Good luck, don't give up, call me in town"*

Red Brakes and Redemption
(Weminuche Detour, Silverton)

This single text pushed us both over Stoney Pass. Brad perked up at the sound of a warm bed. I couldn't wait to eat something real. In fading light, we began to roll away from the last saddle of the day's pass count and downhill on this white and dusty rock road. The grade of the road slipped from slight, to moderate, to extreme. The road switched back countless times and we began passing mining relics of a very large former operation. I was amazed that people climbed this trail in anything but a sturdy four-wheel vehicle. I can't believe they made a living hauling up and down this road at the turn of the century. What could even pull something up this wall? Horses? The first-generation combustion engine? This is the first time I ever experienced honest-to-god brake fade. My fingers and forearms cramped into a claw as I smashed more pressure into my brake levers trying to manage my speed. I started to pump the brakes to create some cooling cycles and cycle colder fluid into the calipers and that worked well. The trail was wildly precarious, I wouldn't attempt driving it in anything but perfect weather. Thick old cables and giant wooden derricks drifted overhead from the days they shuttled suspended ore carts up to the mine openings. We continued down the road barely able to keep ourselves on our bikes. The downhill was demanding in itself. I could easily smell the acrid odor of our brake pad's intense heat. I may have been fabricating the vision, but I could have sworn there was a tinge of red color in my brake rotors. If we had older rim brakes and rubber pads, I'm confident we'd be looking for replacements by the bottom.

We carefully managed the remainder of the descent out of that valley and reached the valley floor. As we rounded the corner onto the dirt road into town, we saw the derelict lower lift building that received the endless stream of ore carts to be processed. It looked like a condemned and dangerous film set. I could imagine the shriek of steam whistles and hissing and clanging of a steam engine as it pulled miles of cable through the house. It must have been some of the worst working conditions in the history of man. Huge iron machines invented to multiply man's force, but no safety invented along with it. This building stood defiant among a wasteland of avalanche debris. It was a near miss that leveled most of our surroundings now including a huge swath of forest and a few residential trailers. It was an eerie sight to glide past. I half expected the ghost of a bearded man to be standing in the upper window.

Finally at the bottom, we could rest. We started a slow recovery pace along mostly flat, slightly downhill dirt road. All kinds of mining relics drifted by on the valley walls above us. First, the equipment itself including more abandoned facilities and machinery and eventually into the forgotten outer reaches of civilization. Eventually the buildings started to shape up, the road below us became heavenly smooth and paved, and the population exploded. We hadn't seen this many people in one spot in five days. We'd made it. Our arrival to Silverton was assured.

I powered my phone up a flood of new information came in. My phone recovered from five days of no connectivity and I sifted through to find the motel confirmation email from Jordan. We looked up the motel's location and rolled into town once more, like cowboys after a cattle drive. The sight of so many people and action was exhilarating. The road was full of noisy and gnarly jeeps and side-by-side off-road vehicles. Live music played from some of the open restaurant doors. The sidewalks were full of tourists enjoying some relief in town after playing in the rough terrain all day. We could smell the pizza and burgers and smoke house and campfires as we biked down main street at dusk.

We pulled into the Prospector Motel's parking lot and tried the office door. It was closed and directed us to another motel nearby to retrieve keys to our room. Neither place was remotely well priced at $100 a night, but this night, it was fully worth it. We entered our room and immediately filled the empty space with our bikes and all of our belongings. Just trying to maneuver inside the cinderblock walls of this ground floor, *Breaking Bad* grade of motel was difficult. It was dry, it was clean, the lights worked, and most importantly, the shower was hot and the beds looked soft (softer than anything we'd slept on since Breckenridge). I didn't dare lay on the bed yet. We stuck our electronics into every outlet in the room, changed clothes in respect of the strangers around us, and headed back out the door in search of any sustenance that could help bring us back to life.

On the way to the motel, we ran into the group of riders we'd camped with the night before and shared the trail with at times during the day. They said they were headed to a pizza place nearby. We too found the place quickly, sat down and promptly ordered huge pizzas and I, a condolence beer. We chatted with the other riders (who's eyes and demeanor appeared equally aimless and flat) about their day, and their plans for the rest of the trip. We were roughly on the same page. I think I remember them wanting to ease out of the trip and stretch the remaining segments into a few more days. Brad and I were more or less over it. We wanted the victory of finishing, right now, hell or high water.

While we were there, feeding our faces, I wanted to find a permanent fix to my ailing rear tire. A quick search on the phone led us to the single bike shop in Silverton. It was just around the corner! I figured they'd be closed in this late hour, so we might head over in the morning, purchase any suitable 29er tire they had, and have it promptly installed and be on our way. I looked up when they would open and to my surprise, *they would not open for another 4 days!* Brad and I were flabbergasted. The only apparent shop in Silverton spends 4 days a week closed up tight. Now, understand, in the end I do not blame the shop owner. I'd rather he/she manipulate their open hours as they please in order to stay in business at all. But at the same time, this wasn't exactly a low traffic area. They were *the only* source of help in the area that held the beginning of some major riding trails. Either way, it was an extra kick in the shorts to read this news. We quickly realized that we'd have to just stick it out with the fix we had in place, and once again, hope. We swallowed that reality and couldn't do much more than shrug.

The others soon called it a night while Brad and I kept working on our plates. There was no point to saving leftovers, I wanted it all inside me! The rest of this night is a blur. I remember finishing every inch of the pizza and my single beer. I recall washing every crevice of my entire body in a blazing hot shower. Jordan and I talked on the phone for a while, but I have no idea what I said or what she said. I remember working on my gear and bike, catching up with routine maintenance and a few small things I'd put off until we had down time. I could only confidently say that I lubed my chain and cleaned my suspension. The remainder is just a vision of my hands in front of me working and toiling on something and my gear spread all around me. I was a robot. My head was in rough shape and I desperately needed some rest. It was hot in our room. We left the window open, unaccustomed to the improved sleeping environment, and soon fell asleep hard.

A New Beginning
(Silverton, Weminuche Detour)

Brad and I slept in just a touch longer than we usually do and found ourselves, once again, in a cold valley. I felt like a completely different person after that long night's sleep and Brad was well improved also. We strapped on our bike shoes, but left our gear behind, and walked down main street again, looking for breakfast. The rowdy town from the night before was still mostly asleep. Only a few early risers in puffy coats (just like us) meandered about, coffee in hand.

We found a historic looking building that now housed a morning cafe. The Brown Bear Cafe treated us well. The waitress was quick and straightforward which I suspect is a holdover from residing in a hardy town such as Silverton. The meal was hot, excellent, and exactly what we needed to kick off the remainder of the trip. If there was something I loved to spend money on during the ride, it was good food. I ordered eggs benedict, a side plate of hash browns, and took the cafe up on their offer for a cinnamon roll + coffee combo. We filled up as much as we dared, left a big tip, and returned back to the room.

We geared up for the day and packed our bikes back into themselves. Squeezing our bikes out the door, we threw our legs over the top and started off the day. It was a short first stint---to the grocery store. We needed to resupply before we continued on and Silverton's tiny grocery store did just fine for us. There we found an interesting new "sweet" line of Clif Bars that we'd never seen before. This was a nice treat to carry for the last few segments. With more packets of pink salmon and instant rice onboard, and fully recharged from the night before, we decided it was time to give the wilderness a punch back. As we left, a family was sitting at patio tables outside of the store. Two elderly parents and a middle aged couple sat in conversation with one another. As we passed by, the younger man's attention drifted to us and I watched him eye our full rig packs. He smiled at me and gave a knowing nod, wishing us luck on the remainder of our journey. We pointed our bikes southwest down Greene street and headed toward paved highway 550 which would guide us up to Molas Pass and the end of the Weminuche Detour.

Leaving the Silverton valley, the town is visible in the distance. Note the lack of any real place to hide while riding up the shoulder of this road

We started up the winding incline along the thinning two-lane highway road. Silverton lay below us in the sunlight to our left and I again imagined what it would have looked like in its mining glory days. Cars and trucks passed by us, some with huge trailers. It was downright dangerous on this road with numerous blind corners with no shoulder to protect us. We stuck our thumbs out again, care free about using help to finish off this detour. We wanted off the road right away!

Many cars passed us by, unwilling to assist, until a man in a pickup truck slowed down next to Brad behind me. A taker! He had an open bed, a big smile, stuck his thumb up back at us---and immediately drove off! "What the f$%& was that?!", Brad fumed. I turned around and saw the truck roaring off and turned further to see what was up. "That a$#hole just stuck his thumb out at us and took off!". We were cussing him out for going the extra mile to taunt a pair of cyclists straining up to the pass. What a jerk, why couldn't he just pass by like the rest of the uninterested? That raised our adrenaline up for a bit but we soon calmed back into our grinding groove. Our thumbs still out, we soon came across a huge, rock star quality RV pulled off into a rare gravel shoulder. A man was at the back with the engine's hatch open turning tools inside. We rode past and asked his companion if she or he needed any help. After a short chat (with our thumbs still out), she revealed that they burst a hose but she thought her husband had it under control. Many cars drove by, squeezing past the RV, but didn't take note of our request for a lift. I remembered the gawking of the drivers from a huge pickup truck and an Astrovan as they went by. We wished the stranded travelers luck and congratulated them on the excellent accommodations they owned, regardless if it was moving or not.

As we started back up the hill I noticed the Astrovan that passed us was making an A-Team style U-turn and flying back down the hill toward us. I called out to Brad, "Hey I think...I think this guy is coming back to us! He just passed us going up the road!". Brad tightened up to me so I could point out the vehicle. Sure enough, we could see him in the distance hurtling back down the road toward us. He slid his coughing and heaving van into the remainder of the gravel patch in front of us. "What's up guys?? You lookin' for a lift?", "Yeah! Do you think you could help? We're just trying to get to the top of the pass without dying", "I thought so! Let's get you guys up there!"

Enter our final trail angel, Brett Lanier. A younger guy, unshaven and smiling, with sandy hair. He and his van were rough around the edges visually, but both full of heart inside. A fellow mountain biker like ourselves, he lives the single life in his van and brings his bike all around the States looking for great trails. For a while we scratched our heads as to how we could fit our rigs inside. He had a full bed setup in the back and his own bike and some storage consuming the usual spaces. I ended up ducking inside and fell backward onto his bed with my bike on top of me. I was doing my best to keep my chain grease and personal grime off of his home, and I figured my back was the cleanest part of my entire existence. Brad crawled into the area between the bed and the driver's seats and knelt beside his upright bike. Brett shoved the door shut, hopped in, and coaxed his van onto the road, missing on one (maybe two) cylinder(s).

We again were on our way to the top of the hill. Brett helped us knock off about 5 miles of treacherous 2-lane road detour shared with high speed vehicles. Opposite of our usual feelings, we were grateful to be off that stretch of pavement. In short order he delivered us to the parking lot at the top of Molas Pass. In the lot we quickly felt welcome with the sight of many other mountain bikers unloading their bikes from various vehicles. They were preparing for the same section of trail we were about to start on and, by the looks of the crowd, it was popular (a good sign).

We thanked Brett up and down and handed him a few bucks for his trouble. He had a classic sticker on his van indicating, *No free rides: Grass, A--, or Gas*, and considering we didn't have the resources to provide the first two options, gas money would have to do. Brett thanked us in return, wished us well, and stuttered off.

God Bless the Trail Builders of Durango
(Segment 25 + 26)

We rolled around the parking lot for a lap taking in the sights of the beautiful overlook of the valley below. It was an amazing sight to behold and seemed extra special as we felt really close to the finish and confident after our night's rest. The valley we'd emerged from was steep and rugged. These little treats help develop the perspective of just how much we have been able to accomplish. You might travel for a long, forested climb before exposing the terrain's view above tree line. Only then do you really appreciate how far you've come, "Man, we were wayyy down there just an hour or two ago. What a push that was". We shamelessly reveled in glory as we accepted the stares of other day-bikers prepping for their ride. Ready again for battle, we followed a trail runner across highway 550 to the start of Segment 27.

In the first quarter mile of the trail, I grew euphoric. The trail was well designed, flowing, and reasonable with obstacles and climbing grades. We didn't have to get off our bikes, even up and over challenging obstacles like a large shelf of rock that presented itself early in the trail. These builders know what they're doing and kept bikers in mind. Brad has reminded me more than once that the last segments of the trail are considered fantastic riding. Some bikers even shuttle it via the narrow-gauge railroad from Durango to make an epic 60-mile loop (On my bucket list)! Seeing how much the trail had changed since the death-march-saw-teeth of trail prior to Silverton made me so confident that we had the remainder of the trail in the bag. The sun was up, the skies clear and deep blue, and I was nearly singing as we pedaled along this shallow climb.

One of the many saddle passes we managed during this portion of the CT

Our progress swelled with our high confidence and manageable trail conditions. We wound along these valley walls that were so starkly different from previous segments. These trails, while still cut directly into the mountainside, were covered in deeply lush vegetation! There were tall thin and thick grasses, exploding wildflowers, and dense fields of strange new plants I'd never seen. These were stalky plants that reached up perfectly vertical to great heights. They were nearly as tall as we were standing on our pedals. As we rode through, their stalks and sturdy wide leaves crowded the trail tight, brushing and zipping along our gear. We probably looked like gophers popping our heads up here and there to see just where we were as we cruised the trail. We continued up in altitude and I became thankful to get out of the dry and dusty harshness of the last 5 arid segments. This area clearly sees more precipitation, or at least humidity, than many other segments of the trail. The dirt was grippy and fun and stayed where it should. If you smiled earlier in the trail, you'd literally get dust in your teeth. Here we smiled and laughed and fist bumped each section that passed, consequence free.

The wildflowers and vegetation were thick and beautiful through this part

We crested the top of a bare and rocky saddle and began our downhill reward to the next climb. As we descended, a rider in bright pink bibs was absolutely charging up to the saddle in the opposite direction. We had heard rumors that a rider was attempting to roll the Colorado Trail northbound in a new time record. We found the man. We later learned his name is Lachlan Morton. He was up and out of his seat, cranking and cranking. He was applying so much torque that while his cadence was low, he and his bike were absolutely flying up the hill. As he rapidly approached, I could see he had tan skin, a rough mustache and beard and long hair. I pulled to the side of the trail to marvel at his pace and let this superhero by. I came to a stop, leaned to my right on one foot like a good little boy, and PSSSSSSHHHHHH!

I'd done it again. The remaining plugs holding my tire in one piece gave way for the last time. They had appeared to have held so well, keeping my rear tire's puncture all the way from segment 17 bone dry. I looked down at my tire in disbelief. I looked back up at the charging record rider not wanting to miss him go by. I looked back down panicking about my leak, looked back up, down. I watched him roll past with a nod. He only had a handlebar bag for his setup and embarrassed us and our Clydesdales with the breeze he created riding by. As expected, no cheering crowds, no time for a chat, here and gone in a flash. He ended up finishing the trail in an absolutely staggering, borderline blasphemous, 3 days and 22 hours. And for salt in the wound, he missed the record by two hours. We watched him push hard up the line we just descended, up and over the saddle, and out of sight.

Brad preparing tools during our blown tire and blown bag breakdowns

I remembered my tire and looked down at its sad shape. I sighed and Brad and I pulled off at the next switchback to handle the situation. He helped me disassemble my rear end to get the tire free from the frame. I deflated it while he fished the tube out of my packs. We had the tire reassembled quickly and the tire bead seated in the rim again. I began pumping and nearly got to full pressure when my blood froze.

On the end of each of the plugs I had inserted earlier, all six or so, was a sharp brass point. I know many of the plugs ejected out of the tire and I couldn't fathom a way for the brass point to get through the tight cut in the tire itself. My eyes widened as I looked at the inflated tire and I thought, *there are sharp metal points digging into this tube right now, in my hands*. It wouldn't last a mile in this condition. More so, I felt like I was handling a bomb and thought they might puncture this fresh and precious tube at any moment. I looked up at Brad and muttered, "We have to do it all again", "What? Why?". I explained the situation and he shrugged in only partial understanding and agreed. Once I got the tube out, I fished around in the puddle of sealing fluid left in the bottom of the open tire and pulled out no less than five points. I opened my palm to Brad and his eyes got wide too, now in full comprehension. "Whatttt thuuuuh F%%%%%ck???". I quietly bagged them into my hip pack and restarted my heart.

I pumped the tire up again once more. It had been a long time since I used a tube tire and my forearm calibration to sense 30psi had faded. I kept cranking until it was good and hard (phrasing*), gave five more pumps for grandma (phrasing*?), and called it square.

At the same time, Brad had been fishing around in his own bags and his lower frame bag blew it's zipper out, identically to my failure near Breckenridge. It had been giving him signs of trouble for some time but we had been trying to baby the bag, hoping to milk it to the end. Every time he opened or closed it, he tried to use the least force possible. He'd carefully align the two seams while he slowly slid the zipper over the teeth. This, no doubt, extended the life of the zipper. The bag finally died right there at the same spot my tire did. We poked a few holes in his bag just like we had done with mine and threaded a length of cord through the holes to 'sew' it partially shut. My bag had already proven this technique to work and we copied it for Brad's failure. Once that was complete, I packed all my tools into my bags again, and sat down in the middle of the trail to clear my mind. We finished segment 25 without any further breakdowns.

Segment 26 kept us near the tree line for a long before we began descending into the forest. The trail was nearing its end and spending time at these altitudes now was emotional and enjoyable. The forests around us were thick pine tree patches dispersed among grassy hill sides and the occasional rocky mountain. This section is faint in my memory but I remember riding along or near ridge lines at high altitude. Most of our views were with unlimited visibility when we could see over the surrounding mountain tops. Endless lush valleys below. I'm not kidding, 100 miles of visibility, easily.

This is what I remember as typical to the later parts of this section

We finally decided to call it a day after Straight Creek. We filled at the creek and passed it by looking for a suitable campsite in the near future. There was a good chance that we could make it far enough today to only spend one additional night on the trail after this one. This convinced us to ride a few more miles into dusk. Straight Creek is marked as the last reliable water source for about 22 miles ahead to Taylor Lake. We realized that we'd have to conserve water and camp "dry". We made the best of the creek by chugging as much water as we could stand and filling every last watertight vessel we had. Brad even stuffed our filtration bag, full to the brim, into his shirt! We started slowly and awkwardly down the trail with our water bags. It was like trying to hold onto eels while riding through the Rockies. We were actively searching for a campsite that was remotely usable. I first spotted a very tight, shoe-horn of a clearing good for only one man in a bivy. "I mean...is that an option?", "No, dude.", Brad replied flatly! We might have been worn but we still had standards dammit! We wiggled down the trail a while longer searching and searching, losing hope. Daylight fades quick when you're not in a tent, funny how that keeps happening.

Brad spotted home for the night as we came around a corner and it was different and beautiful. This wasn't a site like we'd been used to. It was off the trail about 40 feet, on the downslope side. We were already in a heavy forest of thick, insanely branched pines. Their sharp and piercing arms were frozen in place like barbs on giant black snowflakes. The forest floor was covered in green plants. I'm no botanist, but I can describe them as lily pad-like and raised 10 inches or a foot off the forest floor. You more waded through them than walked. The floor of the campsite was dirt, but it was absent of the dry pine needles and poking objects of all the other forested sites we'd slept in so far. This one was soft and mossy, you could walk barefoot with ease. The fallen trees were rotting, not drying. The wind didn't crack, click, and snap the trees above, it was only the sound of wind. It was a bizarre but comfortable welcoming.

I saw in the trail book that there was a campsite marker dictated for further down the trail. I hopped on my bike to go another quarter mile just to ensure we weren't missing out on the most epic campsite of the trip. We weren't, and I returned quickly.

Brad had already gotten the tent out and we did our best to find the most level spot in the site. The whole site sloped and we lived in a funhouse that night. Shortly after, we started our usual routine in camp that we had championed so well over the last two weeks. We ate a huge meal from our full bags from Silverton. It was delicious and I wished I had brought a beer. Without a bath, Brad and I wiped off as best I could and eventually sat down on my pad to stretch while I remembered the day. I was trying to cement these memories in place.

With our closer proximity to civilization now, Brad was able to get some cell service in camp and called home. His voice waivered with emotion as he put his head in his hands and tried to update his wife Elissa. I heard the desperation spill out of him. He wanted to see his family so bad. It made me smile at his love for his family. My own focus fell beyond the dirt in front of me. For most of the trail I was in a high stage of alert, bordering fight or flight. I tackle huge challenges with exponentially increasing amounts of force and, being in that mode most of the trip, I hadn't had much time to zoom out and observe the deeper layers of my own emotions. I realized I was desperate to see my wife again too and emotions flooded into my heart as I heard Brad's unsteady call. We'd done so much and seen so much, but I hadn't done it with her. I don't regret this because Jordan, not being as enthusiastic about riding, would likely have found this project far less than enjoyable. Regardless, Jordan and I do so much together and have conquered so many challenges in life as a team. She's a warrior and my teammate and most importantly the person I love most to share experiences with. I wish she was here with us.

These segments were a huge improvement but weren't without its challenges, either. We still climbed up 3,800 feet of elevation over four major mountain passes. However, this section doesn't stick in my mind as dreadful. I think we were buoyed by the trail design and it allowed us to move through the area at a far more reasonable pace. We spent much time above tree line too with the high point of these segments at 12,310 feet. We were crushing these passes and it felt incredible to accomplish so many miles with so much relative ease. Gone were the days of maximum suffering. Ahead was less than 50 miles remaining of the 550 mile trail. It seemed to be going well. We can really start to taste the finish.

The Mountain is Yielding
(Segment 27 + 28.5)

The second to last day. It wasn't cold this morning! I think the humidity and slightly lower elevations of this area (anything below 11,000 feet is now considered low) helped in the matter and we were appreciative not to be huddled up over the Jetboil dying for coffee. The sun shone through the trees at a shallow angle and lit the forest floor up into brilliance.   The floating leaves glimmered with morning dew. I waded deep into the woods on my own to enjoy a moment of isolated tranquility. And a good poop.

We began with a slow start. Today wasn't a big plan, about twenty miles and 4,000 feet or so would do the job and keep us on track. We had tapered off on the end of our trip intentionally so we didn't have to drag ourselves over the finish. We woke up in good spirits and crushed a big meal of leftovers from last night plus a few additions. Fully laden from Silverton, we had food to spare and thoroughly enjoyed the capability.

We packed up and started off. This segment of trail improved even from the last. I have in my notes, *The trail today was really well designed. Very welcoming gentle traverse with outstanding views. We enjoyed a final sigh of relief that these sections would not kill us.* As described, these trails were filled with meandering traverses of numerous ridgelines near tree line. We'd ride on or near the top of each ridge, hopping from one side of the ridgetop to the other. Each new hop provided us with a new grand view of a different valley. We enjoyed countless moments of, "Wow, Brad, look at this one!" followed by another, "Damn, this is a terrific view!". I could have stopped and camped anywhere in this segment, just to enjoy a full day of the sun's warmth and final views of the CT. We'd been moving so fast and working so hard, our time to sit back and enjoy had been limited.

A typical window into the unlimited visibility of the immense number of valleys below us

I could see the end of our adventure coming and I started to get mixed feelings. A large part of me certainly wanted this experience to conclude. I was hungry, beaten, exhausted, and short tempered. Small hiccups in the trail that tossed me around unexpectedly caused me to roar out loud in disgust. I was done. I missed my wife deeply and wished she was by my side again. On the other hand, this is the most intense test of body and mind I'd ever been subjected to *and I was winning*. That feeling was like a drug. I was surrounded by such formidable and yet enjoyable environments. I deeply love and care for the outdoors. I don't feel at home inside, I feel at home on the porch, no matter the weather. My therapy is a long ride alone, with a long break at a place with a good view. I stare into the distance for a long time, not thinking about anything. When I emerge from the mountains, I'm just a little better inside than I was when I went in. On this trip, I feel I've shaken hands with the Colorado Rockies and we have each other's respect. I don't want to walk away from this friend just yet.

We picked our way down the wildly steep descent to Taylor Lake. It's a small pond nestled in a depression created by the mountain's erosions around us. It was gorgeous. It was a rowdy descent flipping between speed and technicality, but best of all, it was designed with a bike in mind. When we arrived, the lake had nearly a flat entry into the water, and the water was a deep blue-green hue and clear. I almost immediately started a debate up with Brad about whether we should call it a day here to enjoy the site or if we should push on to further prospects. As we laid out the pros and cons, we realized we'd better not screw up the plan this late in the game. Our original idea was to get close to the finish, much less than 20 miles, so if we had any issues on the final day, we could stay on track to meet Jordan and *walk* the hell out of this gauntlet if need be. Stopping here, although beautiful, would leave us exposed again for another night in more alpine elevations. We'd had enough of the cold mornings and lack of sleep. We decided to fill out water and carry on to a campsite lower in elevation.

The outflow from Taylor Lake, where we filled our water

Right after Taylor lake, the trail's angle smoothed into a mild slope. It was fun alpine descending on well-designed trail and relaxing compared to many of the alpine descents so far. As the aspens and then pines whizzed by, we swerved and cut our way down the singletrack all the way to the bottom. Keeping an eye out for future campsites, we searched for the place we'd spend our final night on the trail. On certain lengths of today's trail, the grade became so steep that we had to ease our pace just to keep things in control. However, this section was far easier. We had so much fun dashing through the woods as we descended below tree line for the last time, nearing the city of Durango and the southern terminus.

We came to our final Segment designator: Kennebec Trailhead. We were finally in the last segment of this beautiful, punishing trail. From this point, the trail was almost entirely downhill to the end of the trail. The databook notes that the trail will descend an eye-bulging 6,500 feet while gaining only 1,900. Thinking about those numbers now, even many weeks later, I smile. There was no better home stretch than Segment 28.

A friendly note of encouragement on a sign near the end of the CT

With 22 miles remaining in the ride, we had decided that we still weren't ready to camp and wanted to continue until we had good resources and a walkable distance out. The forest continued as we navigated the switchbacks of this section in the afternoon and evening light. The forest floor was again deep with green vegetation and it crowded the singletrack enough to dab the occasional cluster of leaves as we rode by.

Two waterfalls we saw in the ending segments of the CT, the second had odd white crusted rocks and orange creek bed

We continued on this endless descent and found the area starting to dry out ever so slightly. Our tires splashed through a few creek crossings and even passed a rather large waterfall! The waterfall was a strange sight. All of the rocks around the creek were encrusted white and the river bed was orange. In total, we passed a few smaller waterfalls and creeks with similar white crusting but no waterfall this big. I was sure this was some type of mineral dissolved in the flowing water but wasn't sure if it was naturally occurring or was draining from an abandoned mine in the elevation above. Either way, it made for a cool contrast with the green surroundings. We were able to roll right through this creek and continued on. The wider and better flowing the creeks had become, the drier the surroundings became. After what seemed like such a short time spent descending over the first seven miles, we found our final camp. We rolled down a dry switchback cut into the hillside and spotted the rolling stream, bridge, and campsite below us. We both knew this would be the one.

Our Final Night
(Segment 28)

We pulled in and surveyed the area. It was almost the opposite of what most of our sites had been. This site was closed in by sharply rising terrain and trees in all directions. Our proposed tent site was one of the only level spots that was cleared of brush. If we squeezed in, we could probably fit four tents if they were touching, but not much more than that. An ample and fast flowing stream passed under a hand built wooden bridge that facilitated the CT over the water. A faint trail paralleled the stream away from camp but didn't seem to lead anywhere. As we explored our last night's camp, we were bombarded by flying insects. Initially we were discouraged but soon realized that the bugs weren't biting. We suspected they were only flying ants or gnats or something and they were manageable. Despite the swarming, we were happy to be home!

A few hikers that we passed further up trail went by us on the trail. Maybe it was my trash stash or Brad's chiseled calves, but the hikers poked around a little and then moved on. All except for one. A young woman, about our age, trotted into camp in a near frolic. She was very energetic and had a vibe of a wandering, wide-eyed nature lover with a touch of bravado and...sass? After spending so much time with each other, Brad and I found our new guest a handful! I had a long conversation with her, longer than any other hiker on the trail. I learned about her trip so far, her favorite sections, her reason for the adventure, *her* difficulties in life, *her* gear failures, *her* goals after the trail...I think you get the point. The sentences were flying by as fast as I could catch them! It felt as if she had hiked the entire trail without talking to anyone, and seeing the end was near, had to get it all out on the next person she met! I didn't mind though, I felt the opposite way in that I hadn't heard much from others because we'd been rolling along constantly and didn't spend more than a minute with each person we passed. We weren't traveling at the same speed as the hikers and, therefore, our interactions were fleeting. I got around to telling our stories and we traded our victories and failures on the trail so far. I got the sense that her hike had a very deep meaning for her. She seemed to be at a crossroads in her life. She was juggling higher education, medical issues, and the general direction of her life. She was out on the trail to try to sort it out in her head. I could sympathize because I (and I feel many people) have felt the pressures of at least one of those factors (although I couldn't say I shared those three at the same time!). This hiker reminded me that some people are on this trail for reasons far deeper than mine and I truly hoped they found the peace they searched for.

We rejoined Brad, who had been strangely absent, and we three had dinner together around an old fire ring. We all chatted as we sporked some hot food out of our best packets of dinner selections remaining. We only had fourteen miles left and the excitement to finish was high and all three of us were confident. Our new friend decided she'd set up camp down the faint trail and Brad and I went to our usual nightly chores. We inspected our bikes one last time and I checked the pressure in my rear tube. We took turns standing sentry while the other washed up in the stream--just in case we had to intercept our neighbor from an unwelcome view. Brad ribbed me about our new acquaintance and indicated she might be fishing, and not in the stream. I wasn't sure what to make of the interactions. Nearly ready for bed, Brad and I filled our water bags and brushed our teeth. I crossed paths one or two more times with our neighbor and her glances inched Brad's suspicions into higher probability.

This was our last night on the trail. I surveyed our humble home that we carried all the way from Denver. It was dirty now, just like us, and I was proud. I examined our bikes and gear. They were full of grit and witness marks, worn but unbroken, just like us. I was even prouder. But my greatest pride was in us and what we achieved together. I looked at my trail partner and recalled all of the times we could have quit. I saw him differently now, just a little. I saw confidence and joy in Brad that was less subtle than before. His eyes had begun to express a smirk and hint of swagger. He caught my smiling at him, "...What?". I gazed around our tight corner of Colorado wilderness and looked back at him, "Fourteen to go" and I grinned, "Pretty cool, right?". He smiled and fist bumped me, "F--- yeah it is". My thoughts, exactly.

We took in the surroundings for another few seconds and wiggled into the tent for the last time. The air was warm and bugs were down. I joked with Brad saying that we could quit now and still finish the CT, the shortest way out was the end of the trail! So ready to be done and not so sure at the same time, I ultimately fell asleep smiling to the sound of the stream nearby.

Before I slept, I took out my trail notebook for the last time and scribbled my last entry. I summarized the day as I usually did each night, but this day's submission included something extra (please excuse the curtness of some of the entries, they are an honest symbol of my emotions at the time):

Things I learned on the CT:

It's all in your head
Miners make outrageously bad roads
Don't let your expectations dictate your experience
Your riding partner is always your friend
Breakdowns happen, deal with it
Progress will always be slow, it should be
There is no better water than cold, alpine streams
Take a bath every night if you can
Tent condensation is a real show-stopper
Pick your valley camps wisely
You're not cut out for more than seven days without a real meal--if you intend to stay upbeat
[Focus on] every victory [too], not just defeats
Progress is a victory, it's a win, celebrate it
YOUR WIFE IS YOU'RE EVERYTHING
Don't let other's negativity make you negative
You can only worry so much. If you can't control it, don't worry
F--- bike shops that aren't open four out of seven days a week, including Sunday
Don't bawk at prices if it's what you really need
CO mining towns are really cool (the real ones still left)
I sleep better on my side in a tent
Most of the CT was never meant for bikes
Set your mind to something and don't give up, you will succeed
Appreciate restaurant food, especially good meals in small towns
We all thrive, and suffer, by the sun
Ten-hour bike rides are brutal
7200 feet [of climbing] in one day is brutal
Appreciate having a home
You're stronger than you think you are

*The body can do very much with very little. It will comply
I can scrap most of the internet and social media. Leave
my ability to communicate and learn only*

Finally, to be sure I didn't forget how I felt in this moment, I
added a little self-coaching that I might read down the road
someday. Hopefully Jordan doesn't find this too cheesy:

*Your wife is an enduring, tolerant woman. She's extremely
loving and cares for you dearly. You didn't realize how
much she meant in your life until you were alone and
without distraction. Don't ever take advantage of her and
don't take her sympathy and grace for granted. She holds
your world together, and the sound of her voice breathes
life into you. She can be trusted to save you and just to
help. She's selfless, strong, and smart. You will never find
or need another like her. She enhances your life more than
anything you have. Love her.*

The next page still remains blank.

Bring it Home
(Segment 28)

Dawn broke on a day in which I have no notes. In the chaos of emotions in the last day, I never cracked my notebook to cement the memories. I didn't need to.

We woke in the morning to the same warm air of the night before. I was extremely excited to finish and I could tell Brad was anxious to get going as well. We ate another big breakfast as we threw caution to the wind and finished off our stores. Today would be a balance of time. Jordan was already on the drive to pick us up. She'd left very early in the morning from Denver. I wanted to meter our pace in order to allow her to arrive at the trailhead just slightly before us. That would complete the fully successful finish I had envisioned. By the time we had woken up, we'd have about four hours to finish 4 miles of climbing and then ten miles of true and pure downhill. If the CT hadn't taught me any lessons, I would have said this was to be our easiest day yet!

We packed up camp quickly, despite our extra time. We had become efficient at our engrained routine. We waived goodbye to our camp neighbor as she packed up her tent. We wished her luck and encouraged her to finish strong. Spirits were high as we looked across the creek at the day's task.

Across the bridge was the first 100 yards of trail, cut into the valley wall and inclining away from the creek. Our first climb was steep. We could ride much of it, but not all. This section included a few good pushes as the trail became steep and rocky. The lush greens of the previous descending miles had faded away to the more typical Colorado we knew. As we climbed away from the creek, the trees became ever so slightly more parched and the trail went from soft loam to hard packed, dry dirt. The trail had a steep consequence to our left as we followed the curves of the tight valley walls. We were still in full forests and the branches reached out and dragged over our arms and legs as we did our best to balance along the climbing singletrack. We exchanged between pedaling and pushing, taking breaks often, until we reached the top of the last 1,500 feet of climbing of the 77,000 of the entire Colorado Trail.

We took a longer break at the top of this final push and checked the time. I took my phone out of airplane mode and, closing in on Durango, Jordan's update message came in. She'd meet us around midday. We delayed for just a bit to better match our arrival into Junction Creek, the Southern Terminus. After a bite to eat, we started off again.

Our view near the place we stopped last before descending into Durango

This single downhill helped erase so much pain from the trip. I can hardly describe the joy that went through me as we absolutely crushed this last stretch. The trail was dry and very dusty. It was eroded and dug out around each of the large rocks on the trail. We hammered along at maximum speed. What a rush! I burned every last bit of energy I had as I leaned my bike around each obstacle and slashed each corner. Our bags took a beating and our arms pumped heavily in the massive bumps of the trails. It was an incredible amount of fun. Some sections of the trail smoothed to long, high speed bends and then drove us hard into another endless dusty rock garden. Our bike's suspensions were pushed hard but this is what they were made for. This is what *we* were made for! I grinned and gritted through the dust and jarring.

I felt like we didn't pedal for miles. I'd get a little ahead, Brad would get ahead, we smiled and traded the lead back and forth. We were making great time, flying down this parting gift. I had lost sight of Brad behind me and took a pause for a drink and for him to catch up. A few minutes went by and I started to wonder where he was. After 10 minutes went by, I grew worried! I turned my bike back uphill and double-timed it wondering what was happening. After only a dozen pedal strokes, my phone started ringing! It had been so long since the last time I heard that ringtone that I froze up for a moment in a panic to find my phone and pickup! I finally fumbled the zipper open enough to dig out my phone and saw my partner's name on the screen. "Oh shit" I muttered. I struggled multiple times to swipe the screen to connect, then ripped my gloves off with my teeth. As the phone was in its last ring, I swiped once more and shoved it under my helmet. "BRAD?!", I demanded. "Hey dude...I got a flat. I need the toolkit", he responded coolly. *For f---'s sake*, I thought, and breathed a huge sigh of relief. Sliding down from my panic, I chuckled and told him I was already headed his way. Thank god he wasn't hurt.

In a few minutes time I reversed enough of our descent to find Brad smiling on the edge of the trail, safely in one piece. I shook my head, smiling, "How much further do we have left? Have you looked yet?". "Seven miles!", He responded almost laughing. I couldn't believe it, what luck! Just as we planned, we *could* walk out from here. But we weren't giving in yet! "I broke a spoke", he reported. We both knew that breaking a spoke risks spearing the rim's sealing tape. The tape holds all the tire's pressure in, and it likely had gotten punctured. This is the same issue that occurred to the biking apparition man of the earlier segments. I eyeballed his wheel as I fished out our repair kit from my frame. A crisply snapped spoke laid at an odd angle among the uniform pattern of those still intact. It had done its damage and Brad's tire was totally deflated with a puddle of Stan's fluid in the dirt.

Our only option was to put a tube into his tire. We cracked the tire's bead off the rim, fitted a tube inside, and reassembled the whole thing. When I checked how true his wheel remained, it certainly had a good weave near the broken spoke but was still rideable. All it needed to last was seven more miles! After a quick swig of water, we started off again. We still didn't hold anything back in our descent, the trail was too good! No need to be cautious now. We were so close to the end we could taste the beer and burgers. If we "taco-ed" his wheel in half we wouldn't care. It was more worth it to bomb this run than it was to tip-toe out of the wilderness.

And bomb it we did. Like two luge sleds, nearly out of control, we carved through the trails switchbacks and berms and hopped the rocks in our path. The afternoon sun flashed over us as we rode under the dense forest canopy above. I heard my phone beep again and got the official word. Jordan had made it to the trailhead parking lot and was ready to welcome us in. This was it! This was the end!

We raced down the hill. This descent was huge. Ten miles and thousands of feet down! We tackled it in what felt like an incredible pace. Our final day culminated on the first trailhead structure we spotted through the woods. A miniature roof so common to the information billboards in the National Forests. "Dude this is it!", I screamed. We could see the glint of cars through the trees now, parked around the sign. The end was only a hundred yards away. We pedaled hard for the finish to blast out of the woods triumphant. We reached the edge of the forest, rolled onto pavement, and took in the sight.

"…Is this it?", I asked. We looked around at the plethora of cars and the information sign. No CT marker, no "finish" indicator, no Jordan. "Are we at the wrong goddamn trailhead?!" I wondered aloud, irritated. Brad couldn't make sense of it either.

The short answer is yes, yes, we were. An unbelievably funny face-palm moment to end our epic ride. We'd popped out of the forest one mile before the actual end of the trail. The combination of forks we followed lead us to the *Pine Junction Campground* instead of the *Pine Junction Trailhead*. We were such nimrods. Oh well, we didn't care! We'd already started down the road to try to find some kind of directional information when we spotted the remaining trail in the gulley off our right. We were still headed in the right direction, and were coasting down the forest road with the last mile of the CT parallel to us, just fifty yards to our right. Brad said that after more than 500 miles, that was close enough for him. We zipped down the pavement effortlessly and pulled into the next parking lot on our right yelling and shouting our victory.

This time we weren't mistaken. We both rolled right up to the end of the trail. This information sign said *The Colorado Trail* in large font. It was the end. My gorgeous wife hopped out of her car as we circled the parking lot in a victory lap. "Hi guys!!", she yelled. She was beaming from ear to ear, as was I. I stopped and dropped my bike and gave her the grimiest hug she's probably ever encountered. Fourteen days of trail worn into my skin and hair. More than fourteen days without a shave. I was a malnourished, stinky, grungy mess. She kissed me hard anyway. I hugged her so tight and her body in my arms filled me with happiness. I hugged Brad and high-fived him in our victory.

I don't know what else we talked about the entire time we spent in the lot. All I do remember is the grins, laughs, happy sighs, and my brimming with emotion. We started to shed our gear into the car. When the trunk opened, Jordan grabbed two bottles of champagne out of a box. "Champagne finish?", She asked. We both immediately agreed and unfoiled our bottles as we walked over to the sign again. Jordan recorded a video as we blew the corks off, made the bottle neck into a nozzle with our thumbs, and properly hosed each other off in a wild celebration of foamy spray. I raised the bottle over my head and began dumping it into my mouth. I immediately choked on the intensity of the suds and bent over to catch my breath. Brad was still spraying me head to toe. It was awesome. I've watched that video over and over since, just to remember how absolutely happy we were.

I'd brought a tote bin with a fresh change of clothes to wear. We would then place all of our nasty clothes and underwear from the ride into the bin to keep it from stinking the car. My fear was on the way home we'd return from a bathroom break, open the doors, and the stench from our riding gear in the hot car would kill each of us. The bin worked great, though! We wiped the stickiness of the champagne and grime of the day and changed into our new outfits. We removed our frame bags off the bike and loaded the naked skeletons onto the rack of the car. They had seen their last foot of the trail and, like heroes, would be carried home. There was only two times I expected to be putting *this* bike on *this* rack. We would have either bailed off the trail, or we would have finished it. I was proud to place my bike on the rack in victory. It was a good moment of finality.

We boarded the car, and for the first time in a long time, we drove in windless, effortless, climate-controlled comfort. We pulled out of the trailhead parking lot and made our way down the forest road. The signs of civilization quickly increased from residences to businesses to full strip malls and a full-blown city. We had arrived in Durango. We headed toward *Ska Brewing* for a beer and a bite, an excellent choice suggested by Brad.

We walked inside and ordered burgers over the counter and a few beers. We sat down at the picnic tables and chowed down. It was one of the best meals of my life and the beers were totally satisfying. Jordan smiled and laughed at our wild descriptions of the trail as we chatted about everything that happened.

When we finished our beers, Jordan delivered us home uneventfully. During the six-hour drive, I remember watching the mountain ranges pass by in the distance and thinking,

"I cannot believe I just rode a bike through all of that".

Epilogue

Thanks

It's hard to imagine this adventure without the willingness of my wife, Jordan. I have praised her in this text often and she deserves every one. She constantly attempts to improve me as a person, and I constantly test her patience. Remember, I burnt both weeks of my annual vacation allotment to accomplish this ride. She was not only willing to let this project divert enormous attention, she was also willing to give up a major vacation she would have otherwise had. In so many ways, more than I could list, I owe her back.

My riding partner Brad deserves commendation next. I'm so thankful to have someone like him in my life to help me explore the edges of the comfort zone. Day after day, Brad delivered what was required and his commitment was instrumental in our finish. It took the both of us to have the confidence and grit to finish this task. More than once he picked me up when I was down, and I'm happy Brad was my partner that I counted on. When the going got far tougher than we expected, he didn't give up. I will always hold our memories in high regard.

Elissa (and Kennedy) sacrificed a great deal for this too. Both of our spouses were stretched thin at times. Elissa had the additional load of watching Kennedy, their toddler, during the ride. I don't yet know what kind of strain that induces, but I can respect that it's not small. Elissa not only committed to Brad's dream of completing the trail, she held down the fort in his absence, *while pregnant with their next child*. I'm very proud and thankful of her too.

Next, is Spot Bikes. Spot is a boutique brand of premium, highly refined bikes of many types. The Mayhem 130 29 they sold me was no exception and it stood the ultimate test. I look forward to owning that bike for a long, long time. The shop guys have always treated me well and charged me a fair price for everything I've asked.

The Colorado Trail Foundation and volunteers are the shepherds of this journey. They spend countless, thankless hours hauling into the backcountry to maintain and repair trail so that people can safely find their way through the greatest adventure of their lives. Although we may disagree on the shape the trail should assume, there is no question that what they've built is truly special, marvelous, and enduring.   I may never meet the generations of folks that have put a pick to stone on that trail. I hope they know that they've helped thousands continue to enjoy the outdoors.

After effects Body + Bike

Brad told me he lost about 10 pounds in the two-week ride. I myself lost about 8 and I'm not sure I had that much to lose! We knew it was coming because we had been slowly cinching in our riding shorts as the days passed. Everything we wore was baggier and I was starting to have trouble getting my shorts past the nose of my bike seat without hanging up. Jordan was pretty shocked when she saw me with my shirt off for the first time post-ride. She declared, "We need to get you something to eat" and deemed me in the "unhealthily skinny" category. Surprisingly, my muscles felt fine. I could tell I had done some work but I'd put my soreness at a 3 or 4 out of 10. I attribute this to our constant, slow-burn pace.

It saved us from overwork and injury. My saddle sores and gut were my two biggest complaints after the ride. The sores took about two weeks to fully heal. I never had a major issue with chafing as much as I did plain old squashing of tissue. The peak of the pain was at the first third of the ride. I think my ass just died after that and we carried on. My gut and calorie consumption, however, was the real challenge. I was seriously emaciated. At the end of the ride, I would consume so much food per sitting that I would be awfully uncomfortable. I'd be in physical pain for hours until my stomach caught up with the voluntary force-feeding. This coupled with hunger pangs between meals that were a carryover from the trail. Sharp cramps just below my sternum hit every few minutes. It took me more than a month or more before I felt my body was fully acclimated to normal life and diet again. I thank Jordan here too for supplying our household with such great ingredients in our diet plan. Finally, I had scraped the hair and skin off the inside of both calves due to their intermittent rubbing on the frame bags. I'm happy to report the bald spots have regrown.

Regarding our bikes, I ended up with a tube in the rear tire and rear tire tread at about 50% of its lifespan remaining. I wore in lots of shine on the 1 gear and right side of the chainring as 70,000 ft of climbing rubbed a familiar path through the drivetrain. There was a lot of playa dust in every crevice of the bike, literally all possible real estate had some grit. Both wheels could benefit from a minor truing. Finally, the derailleur suffered some slight clicks and missed shifts, and my suspension had a touch of stiction. Spot, the makers of my bike, took care of both of these issues when I dropped it off for service.

In the months after our ride, I'm thrilled to say that it doesn't feel like my bike has even done the trip! What a testament to solid design.

What Struggled on the Trail

I have mixed feelings about my Dynaplug tubeless plugging kit. I spoke with the makers of the kit after the ride and agree with them on many things. First, plugging tires isn't an exact science. Each puncture is a little different and it's next to impossible to make a solution for each. I think in the end I was on the unlucky side of that equation and have to admit it was my first time ever using the kit. At the same time, the plugs weren't a full miracle, but I don't think they could be. I still carry the kit in my bag. It, and their supportive staff, deserve a second chance.

The additional "Quasi" handlebar bag needed the axe before we even left. We carried too much. All of the additional camera mounts, fishing gear, etc. didn't stand a chance. Every possible fraction of an ounce should be considered before being included.

Sludgy super calorie food might sound like a good way to increase your calorie-ounce ratio but be careful not to kick yourself off your own game.

Keep your tent ventilated. Tent moisture was a real progress stopper.

The Topeak Midloader bag zippers proved unreliable. The bag themselves are of sturdy construction. It's a shame that the zippers let the bags down. Topeak replaced both of our bags under warranty. The Front and Backloader bags worked quite well, in contrast.

I didn't even crack open the trail maps during the entire ride. We used the MTBProject app almost exclusively with backup on the COTrex app, loaded offline onto both our phones. As double-redundancy, I also carried a Garmin InReach (which I love) that also had the CT line loaded in it. The larger trail information book was useful in planning but left at home, and the smaller waterproof data book was extensively used on the trail. I'm a loyal cartography enthusiast, so I wouldn't have ditched the maps if I had to do it again. But, I'd also understand if others chose not to bring them, as sacrilege as that is.

Finally, I should have better cleaned my phone out for storage of video and photos. I had to do a wild shuffle of microSD cards between my Rylo camera and my phone trying to provide enough space for all of the footage. This critically zapped my electronic's battery life. My later-footage frequency dwindled to try to conserve space and energy because of this.

Parting Thoughts

My adventure is not for everyone. But *adventure* is for everyone, in my opinion. Take one step outside of normal. Just get started in the right direction to better yourself, your life, and those around you. Go the extra mile and share it with your peers. Your adventure doesn't need to be extreme, or wild, or intense, or big, or outdoors, or relatable, or proper. It just needs to be yours.

 - Matt

"Because in the end, you won't remember the time you spent working in the office or mowing your lawn. **Climb that goddamn mountain.**"

Made in the USA
Monee, IL
26 July 2020

37036131R00118